A Scientific Approach to More Biblical Mysteries

A Scientific Approach to More Biblical Mysteries

by
Robert W. Faid

New Leaf Press

First printing: March 1995
Second printing: September 1996

Copyright © 1994 by New Leaf Press. All rights reserved.
Printed in the United States of America. No part of this book
may be used or reproduced in any manner whatsoever
without written permission of the publisher, except in the
case of brief quotations in articles and reviews. For information write: New Leaf Press, Inc., P.O. Box 726, Green
Forest, AR 72638.

ISBN: 0-89221-283-7
Library of Congress Catalog Number: 94-69838

All Scripture is from the King James Version of the Bible.

For my children
Brent and Robyn,

my son-in-law, Zac,

and my grandchildren,
Austin, Martin, Timothy,
Ruth, and Michelle

Contents

Preface

As a scientist who is also a Christian, I am tremendously interested in truth. My scientific background forces me to seek it, my faith as a Christian demands it, and as an author I am compelled to write it. But sometimes truth disturbs people very much, especially when it runs counter to what they have been taught all their lives by men and women they respect.

Nothing in this book contradicts the essential facts of our Christian faith. Jesus Christ is the Son of the living God, was crucified and buried, and arose from the dead. What Jesus is and what He did is the important and indisputable basis of our faith.

But there are other events in the Bible having nothing to do with these essentials, which through time have somehow been distorted. What the Bible says is correct, but man's interpretation of what actually took place sometimes is not. Through time, this distortion of events has become so ingrained in our minds that it seems sacrilegious to even question them.

But these are the very points which skeptics point to when they question our Christian faith. In order to successfully answer the unbeliever when our faith is put on the line, we must know how to answer these difficult questions. Jesus gave us His commandment in the Great Commission — to bring light to those who walk in darkness and truth to those who are bound by Satan's lies. In order to accomplish this, we ourselves must know the truth.

Jesus spoke many times about truth. He said that His followers would know the truth and that "the truth shall make you free" (John 8:32).

I sincerely hope that the reader of this book will not only

find what it contains interesting and informative, but that it will better enable them to fulfill the Great Commission which our Lord commanded of each one of us. I am sure that you, like me, are interested only in the truth that our Saviour spoke of, the truth which makes us truly free.

1

Has Noah's Ark Been Found?

One of the most controversial narratives in the Old Testament is the story of Noah and his huge ark on which he and his family and the animals rode out the great flood to repopulate the world. Skeptics have attacked this biblical account by claiming that the great Flood never happened, or if it did it was a local phenomenon and not a worldwide disaster. It is not within the scope of this chapter to offer all of the evidence of Noah's worldwide flood. This has been dealt with in detail in a previous book.[1]

But other arguments raised by scoffers include their skepticism about the ark being capable of carrying mating pairs of all the animals required to renew life on the earth after the waters of the Flood subsided. And if Noah had actually constructed such a ship, it could not possibly have withstood the torrents of water let loose by the Flood described in Genesis for such a period of time.

They also claim that Noah and his three sons would have been incapable of constructing a ship of the dimensions given in Genesis. After all, they claim, the technology of Noah's time was extremely primitive. Even though the Bible tells us that God gave Noah 120 years to construct this huge ship, skeptics scoff at Noah's ability to actually build a vessel so large. After all, they claim, it was not until the eighteenth century A.D. that ships as large as the ark were capable of being constructed.

Skeptics also state that it is impossible for anyone to prove that such a ship as Noah's ark actually existed, for it was so far back in time that no remains of the vessel could possibly be found to substantiate the biblical story. These are some of the questions which scoffers have raised which will be answered in this chapter.

Could the Ark Really Have Held All Those Animals?

It was God who gave Noah the plans and specifications for the ark. But could such a ship have held all the animals necessary to re-populate the earth after the Flood had destroyed all life? Just how large was this vessel?

"And this is the fashion which thou shalt make it of: The length of the ark shall be three hundred cubits, the breadth of it fifty cubits, and the height of it thirty cubits" (Gen. 6:15).

A cubit was the distance from the tip of a man's elbow to the end of the middle finger of his hand. A cubit was therefore approximately 18 inches, or one and a half feet. The ark would have been 450 feet long, 75 feet wide, and 45 feet high.

If we multiply these dimensions together we get a total volume inside the ark of about 1,518,750 cubic feet. Just how many animals could Noah have fit into this space? God also specified that there would be three stories, or decks, in the ark.

"A window shalt thou make to the ark, and in a cubit shalt thou finish it above; and the door of the ark shalt thou set in the side thereof; with lower, second, and third stories shalt thou make it" (Gen. 6:16).

So we have a three-story ark with a volume of over one and a half million cubic feet inside. How many different species of animals would Noah have had to bring into the ark in order to preserve this life to re-populate the earth?

In his book, *Principles of Systematic Zoology*, Ernst Mayr has provided a table of the number of animal species.

Mammals - 3,700
Birds - 8,600
Reptiles - 6,300
Amphibians - 2,500
Fish - 20,600
Tunicates, etc. - 1,325
Echinoderms - 6,000
Arthopods - 838,000
Mollusks - 107,250

Worms, etc. - 39,450
Coelenterates, etc. - 5,380
Sponges - 4,800
Protozoans - 28,400
Total Animals - 1,072,300[2]

But not all of these animals would need the ark to survive the Flood. It was only the land animals which would need the protection of the ark to carry them through the great Flood. Certainly, fish and amphibians could survive, as could the mollusks, tunicates, echinoderms, sponges, coelterates, protozoans, and most of the species of worms and arthropods. This really narrows down the number of animals Noah would have to transport on the ark primarily to land mammals and reptiles and some insects.

Actually, it is estimated by LaHaye and Morris that no more than 35,000 vertebrates would have had to have been taken aboard the ark. To be on the safe side, and to satisfy skeptics, they use as a basis for calculation 50,000 land animals. Most animals are small, of lesser size than a sheep. How many animals, therefore, the size of a sheep would the ark be capable of carrying?

Sheep are sometimes transported today in railway stock cars. A two-decked railway stock car is capable of carrying 240 sheep in its 2,670 cubic foot capacity. LaHaye and Morris divided the volume of a standard railway stock car into the volume of the ark. They found that Noah's ark was equivalent to 569 standard railway stock cars.

LaHaye and Morris note that since one car is capable of holding 240 animals the size of a sheep, all of the animals that Noah would have had to accomodate aboard the ark would take up only about 36 percent of the ark's capacity. They write, "In other words, assuming a minimal size for the ark and a maximum number of animals, we find that the ark was not too small for the task, as many have claimed."[3]

Could the Ark Have Survived the Flood?

In Noah's time, the art of shipbuilding was probably confined to the construction of raft-like structures used to float lazily down the rivers or small and very primitive boats used by fishermen. Certainly nothing of the size of the ark had ever been constructed previously. Since the Genesis account of the great Flood suggests that it was a very violent release of water which would have resulted in huge waves and powerful currents, would this craft have been capable of withstanding such conditions without capsizing?

It is certainly true that nothing like it had ever been built before. The ark built by Noah and his three sons was a monstrous thing, over 300 feet long. Roman ships of about 50 B.C. were only about 150 feet long, half the length of Noah's ship. Admiral Nelson's flagship, *Victory*, built in the eighteenth century, was only 186 feet in length. Was this craft capable of withstanding the force of water which was generated by the opening of the "fountains of the deep?"

Yes, it was! When naval architects examined the plans for Noah's ark and built scale models for testing, they found that it was ideally suited for its task. This simply designed vessel was perfect for riding out the flood and withstanding the forces of water which must have accompanied it. It has been found to exhibit stability under the most severe conditions possible without capsizing. The experts are amazed at the perfection of its design. But, of course, we know who the Designer really was.

Not only was the ark capable of carrying all the animals required for re-population of the earth, its design was absolutely perfect to ride out the greatest storm the world has ever seen. But could a ship of this size actually have been constructed by four men — Noah and his three sons Shem, Ham, and Japheth? Let us look at some calculations and decide for ourselves.

Could the Ark Have Really Been Constructed?

Nothing like the ark had ever been built before! It was an immense construction project. Could Noah and his three sons actually have accomplished this? True, they had 120 years in which to complete it, but consider the enormity of what they would have had to do.

Noah could not have picked up the telephone and called the local lumberyard to obtain the wood. Each beam, each piece of planking, would have had to have been hewn from a log. And each log required these men to cut down a tree, haul it to their work area, saw or cut it with axes into the appropriate size and shape, then plane and dress it to fit within strict dimensional tolerances. Could four men have really constructed such a huge vessel in this fashion?

LaHaye and Morris have estimated that four men could only have cut and dressed and installed about 15 cubic feet of lumber per day.[4] Working six days each week, 52 weeks per year, Noah and his sons could have cut, dressed, and installed 4,680 cubic feet of wood in a year's time.

Since it may be estimated that the ark would require 380,000 cubic feet of wood, Noah and his sons could have accomplished this feat in only 81 years. There would have been 39 years left over. With the added time required to caulk the seams with pitch within and without, build any necessary cages, etc, and to warn their neighbors of the impending disaster to come, the interval of 120 years between God's order to build the ark and its completion would have been more than sufficient.

Has Noah's Lost Ark Been Found?

No! Noah's "lost" ark has not been found! The reason is very simple. It was never "lost" in the first place! People from early antiquity have always known where it was — and still is — located.

The earliest record of the whereabouts of the ark dates all the way back to about 275 B.C. An early historian named Berosus knew exactly where the ark was. Although his original work, *History of Babylonia,* has been lost, excerpts from his work have been quoted by other ancient writers who had access to his writings. Alexander Polyhistor, who lived in the last century B.C. quotes Berosus as follows: "But of this ship that grounded in Armenia some part still remains in the mountains of the Gordyaeans in Armenia, and some still get pitch from the ship by scraping it off and use it for amulets."[5]

In the same work, Berosus is again quoted by Polyhistor, "But the vessel in Armenia furnished the inhabitants with wooden amulets to ward off evil."[6]

Josephus wrote in *The Antiquity of the Jews,* "After this the ark rested on the top of a certain mountain in Armenia. . . . However, the Armenians call this place *The Place of Descent;* for the ark being saved in that place, its remains are shown there by the inhabitants to this day. Now all the writers of barbarian histories make mention of this flood and of this ark; among whom is Berosus the Chaldean; for when he is describing the circumstances of the flood, he goes on thus: 'It is said that there is still some part of this ship in Armenia, at the mountain of the Cordyaeans; and that some people carry off pieces of bitumen, which they take away, and use chiefly as amulets for the averting of mischiefs.' Hieronymus, the Egyptian, also, who wrote the Phoenician Antiquities, Mnaseas, and a great many more, make mention of the same. Nay, Nicholas of Damascus, in his ninety-sixth book, hath a particular relation about them, where he speaks thus: 'There is a great mountain in Armenia, over Minyas, called Baris, upon which it is reported that many who fled at the time of the Deluge were saved; and that one who was carried in an ark came on shore on the top of it; and that the remains of the timber were a great while preserved.' "[7]

Josephus also makes mention of the remains of the ark being visible in his own time, in the first century A.D. He writes, "But when Monobazus was grown old, and saw that he had but a little time to live, he had a mind to come to the sight of his son before he died. So he sent for him, and embraced him after the most affectionate manner, and bestowed on him the country called Carrae; it was a soil that bare amomum in great plenty: there was also in it the remains of that ark, wherein it is related that Noah escaped the deluge, and where they are still shewn to such as are desirous to see them."[8]

The next recorded mention of the existence of Noah's ark was made by Theophilus of Antioch in A.D. 180. "And of the ark, the remains are to this day to be seen in the Arabian mountains."[9]

Epiphanius of Salamis (A.D. 315 to 403) asked the question, "Do you seriously suppose that we are unable to prove our point, when even to this day the remains of Noah's ark are shown in the country of the Kurds?"

John Chrysostom (about A.D. 345 to 407) wrote, "Do not the mountains of Armenia testify to it, where the ark rested? And are not the remains of the ark preserved there to this very day for our admonition?"

In about A.D. 610, Isidore of Seville makes mention of Noah's ark in his *Etymologies*. "Ararat is a mountain in

Armenia, where the historians testify that the ark came to rest after the Flood. So even to this day wood remains of it are to be seen there."[10]

Even the explorer Marco Polo gives testimony to Mt. Ararat as the site where the ark came to rest. He traveled through Armenia in about A.D.1271 and dictated *The Book of Marco Polo* to a fellow inmate while a prisoner in Genoa in about 1298. He wrote, "In the central part of Armenia stands an exceedingly large and high mountain, upon which, it is said, the ark of Noah rested, and for this it is termed the mountain of the ark."[11]

A monk named Jehan Haithon wrote an interesting comment in A.D. 1254, "Upon the snows of Ararat a black speck is visible at all times: this is Noah's ark."[12]

There are sporadic reports concerning the ark during the Middle Ages, none of which is very specific. It seemed as though the ark had disappeared from the mind and settled into the dust of obscurity. But in 1840 an event occurred which again thrust the great vessel of Noah into the forefront.

The Earthquake of 1840

On June 20, 1840, a powerful earthquake struck Mt. Ararat which opened up a massive section of the upper portion of the mountain. Ararat lies along an active seismic fault line and the mountain is actually a volcano, attested to by the extensive lava build up, thousands of feet thick in some places, on its slopes.

The earthquake of 1840 and the subsequent avalanche of rock, mud, and melted water from the ice pack destroyed the village of Ahora. It also either created or exposed a huge gorge in the side of the mountain.

Tradition has it that it was at Ahora where Noah saw the rainbow after the Flood, God's "bow in the sky" by which He promised never to again destroy the earth by water. It was here at Ahora, according to local legend, that Noah built the altar to God, and offered a sacrifice of thanks for His protection and deliverance through the long ordeal. Tradition also states that it was here that Noah planted his first vineyard. All traces of the town were obliterated by the earthquake.

But the disaster may have accomplished something else. Five thousand years of debris were cleared from this portion of Ararat, and perhaps again exposed the ark to view high up at about 14,000 feet near its summit. For it is remarkable that since this event, sightings of the ship have greatly increased. And by virtue of a second natural disaster in 1883, interest was again stimulated in finding the ark.

The Second Earthquake

On May 2, 1883, another earthquake struck Mt. Ararat. Not as powerful as the 1840 shock, it nevertheless was strong enough to shake the mountain violently and destroy many of the small villages on its slopes. This incident caused the Turkish government to send out an investigative team to survey the damage. What this team found was to shock the world. They accidentally stumbled upon Noah's ark.

A newspaper report of the startling discovery states that the team came upon a gigantic structure of very dark wood, embedded in a glacier, with one end protruding 20 to 30 feet. It was made of wood not grown in that region and was in a good state of preservation, constructed of great strength, and seemed to be painted with a dark brown pigment.

A part of this structure had been broken, probably from being carried down the glacier. It was estimated to be 40 or 50 feet in height, but its length could not be determined because it was embedded solidly in the ice of the glacier.

Through one of the broken corners, they were able to enter the structure for a short distance, finding the interior partitioned off into compartments about 12 or 15 feet high. They could enter only three of these compartments, for the rest of the structure was filled with ice.[13]

Despite the newspaper reports of the finding of Noah's ark, the Turkish government would not release the official report of the team. Probably, it still lies buried in official files somewhere.

Since that time there have been numerous reports, from Russian soldiers in the First World War, American airmen in World War II, and civilians, of both sightings and actual visits to the ark. Several accounts given by local inhabitants of the area detail visits to the great ship, being taken there by relatives when they were young boys.

Few of these accounts can be verified, but most of them strangely agree in details. Most agree that the ark is embedded in a glacier and lies in a general north-south direction. Their estimates of the height, length, and width agree, as does their description of the wood and its condition. All seem to tell of an opening in the structure with the door missing. Many describe a small pond just below where the structure juts from the glacier.

Richard Bright, in his book, *The Ark, A Reality?* takes a penetrating look at the details of these sightings, comparing them with weather measurements in the year they were reported. His analysis indicates that these people did, indeed, see something and what they saw fits what the Bible tells us about the ark. Richard also gives in detail all of the current information concerning past and recent searches on Ararat, including those in which he has personally been involved. I highly recommend the interested reader to obtain a copy of this excellent book.[14]

Is the Ark Really There?

Let's examine this question with a bit of healthy scientific skepticism. First, would a wooden structure be able to survive for perhaps as long as 10,000 years? Would it not have decayed and rotted by now?

Not long ago the very well-preserved remains of a man were found frozen in the Alps. When the body was removed from the solid ice in which it had been encased, scientists were both shocked and delighted. This was the body of a man who had lived several *thousand* years ago. Not only were his clothing, his bow and arrows, leather quiver, and other items in almost perfectly preserved condition, but the tissue and flesh had also been well preserved by his frozen environment.

Is it not reasonable, then, to believe that if the leather, cloth, and even the flesh of a man can be kept from decay for thousands of years by being encased in solid ice, *a wooden structure* could also be preserved in the same way? Mount Ararat is 17,000 feet above sea level. Much of this mountain is covered by glacial ice which never melts. If the ark has been encased in ice, would there have been any more deterioration of the wooden planks and beams than of the body of the man found locked in the glacier in the Alps?

The ark *could* still be in much the same condition as the

day when it came to rest on the top of the mountain. Certainly, if a man's flesh can survive without decomposition for thousands of years, then it is not unreasonable to expect heavy wooden beams and planks to have also survived.

Next we must consider how the structure, which has reportedly been seen by so many people, wound up on top of a high mountain. If this structure is a ship, which it resembles, there are only three possibilities.

1. It was constructed there.

2. It was built when the land area on which it rests was lower, then the earth rose as the mountain was formed.

3. It was constructed somewhere else, and it *floated* to its present position.

We will consider each of these possibilities in turn.

First, a wooden structure could not have been built on top of Mount Ararat because there are no trees at that elevation. In fact, the position where the structure has been reported is thousands of feet above the tree line. It is also inconceivable that timbers could have been carried to this location from farther down on the mountain. It is a difficult climb for a man carrying only a backpack. Heavy loads such as the massive timbers which form this structure could in no way have been transported up the steep slopes of Mount Ararat.

Next, could the structure have been built before the land mass rose to form the mountain. Mount Ararat is a volcano. Lava flows, some thousands of feet deep, are to be seen on its sides. Certainly, if the land mass rose as a result of volcanic action, the wood of this structure would have long since been destroyed by the molten lava. And why would anyone construct such a large ship where there was no river or sea for its use?

The third possibility is that this vessel was constructed somewhere else and *floated* to its present location. That, of course, would mean that the water would have had to cover the location where it rests today, or even higher, for there is evidence that the structure has been carried down the mountain by the glacier.

This means that there had to be a flood of unimaginable magnitude. Was there such a catastrophic event? Well, in the traditions of over 200 groups of native cultures, covering the

Middle East, Africa, Asia, the islands of the Pacific, and both North and South America, there are traditions which include a great flood far back in their history.[15] These flood traditions are markedly similar in many respects, with a boat figuring prominently in most of them, a few survivors of the human race on board, and the majority even include the saving of animals in this boat along with the human beings. I will not go into the geological evidence for the great Flood but this is covered in many books on this subject.

Is the structure on top of Mount Ararat really and truly the ark which Noah built? Is it the boat of Scripture on which eight persons and pairs of all species of land animals were saved from destruction? What is the evidence for this structure actually being Noah's ark?

Whether you personally believe the story in Genesis or not, don't you think that it is highly unusual that this particular mountain is where all of these reports of sightings have occurred? But this is exactly where the Bible tells us that Noah's boat rested after the great Flood.

"And the ark rested in the seventh month, on the seventeenth day of the month, upon the mountains of Ararat" (Gen. 8:4).

Is it not strange that from far back in history, at least as far back as 200 B.C., there are written records of Noah's ark being seen on a mountain by the name of Ararat — exactly where the Bible says that it came to rest?

And is it not quite unusual that even in our own time, there are not only reports of persons who have seen, some even visited, this wooden structure on the side of this very same mountain?

Has Noah's ark really been discovered?

No!

It was never lost! It's still there, in the same place that God in His Word has told us it was. It rests today, just as it did in Noah's time — ". . . upon the mountains of Ararat."

The government of Turkey has not been cooperative in allowing scientists access to the area where the ark rests. In fact, one might suspect that they really do not want the truth known and declared to the world. What a stunning blow to atheism this would be! What a dramatic confirmation of the validity and accuracy of God's Word this would be to an unbeliving world!

I firmly believe that the time will come when scientists will be allowed to examine this ancient vessel lying on the slopes of Mount Ararat. This will come, I am convinced, in God's perfect timing and as perhaps a final testimony to unbelievers before this age comes to a close with the return of Jesus Christ.

2

What Is God's Real Name? What Did Mary Call Jesus?

The Old Testament begins in Genesis 1:1 with a profound statement: "In the beginning God created the heavens and the earth."

The Hebrew word used here for God is אֱלֹהִים.

It is pronounced *Elohim*. It is the Hebrew word which means God. It is not God's name, it is really a title. In Genesis 1:1, God is simply stating what He, as God, did in the beginning of time. He created the heavens and the earth.

The word *Elohim* is a term used in the ordinary sense and can actually mean any god, the true God, or the false gods of pagan religions. The word *El* can also mean any god. God revealed himself to Abram in Genesis 17:1 as El Shaddai, אֵל שַׁדַּי. This means "God Almighty."

It would not be until Moses met God in the flames of the bush that burned, but was not consumed, that God would reveal His actual name to His people.

The name of God is contained over 5,500 times in the Old Testament. In our English Bible translations, this name is usually rendered as Jehovah. But do you know that Jehovah as the name of God was totally unknown until about A.D. 700 when the Masorites instituted the use of vowel points to aid in the pronunciation of Hebrew words?

The name of God was considered so sacred by the Hebrews that they refused to pronounce it. Instead, they substituted the Hebrew word *adonai*, meaning "Lord," whenever they came to God's name in Scripture.

In Hebrew, only consonants are written. Until the Masorites began using signs to indicate which vowels to use with the written consonants, a Hebrew student would have had to recognize the word only from the consonants and use the proper vowel sounds by memory.

After the Jews were dispersed in A.D. 70, and the temple was destroyed in Jerusalem, the people were scattered. The language of Hebrew quickly began to decline in use among those who were in other lands. Jews in Egypt had long spoken Greek, and those who were displaced to various other nations gradually adopted that country's language. Hebrew was fast becoming a "lost language."

The Masorites were concerned about this. The meaning of many Hebrew words had already been lost irretrievably. These scholars invented a system of signs, which signified the proper vowel sound to be used. These were placed above or below the Hebrew consonants as a guide to the proper pronunciation of the word.

This worked extremely well, and we owe the Masorites a debt of gratitude for their preservation of much of the biblical Hebrew we have today. But there was one big problem. What were they to do with the unutterable name of God?

This was solved by adding the vowel points taken from the Hebrew word "Lord" and placing them on the Hebrew consonants comprising God's name. They made one change, however, by using the vowel sign for "e" in place of the one for an "a" in the first syllable. The Masorites were afraid that anyone seeing the syllable "ya" would inadvertently blurt out the sacred name by mistake. This, they reasoned, would prompt Jews to say "adonai" instead of pronouncing God's real name which they were forbidden to utter.

In the Greek language Old Testament, the translators have used the terminology "the Being" as God's name, for the vagueness of the Hebrew tense used could be translated in several ways. In many English Bibles this is rendered "I Am That I Am."

But when the Old Testament was finally translated into languages other than Hebrew, Greek, and Latin, translators looked at the consonants and vowel points placed by the Masorites and came up with an entirely new name for God. One of the first translations, in German, used the name

Jehovah. Other language translations followed this and we have had Jehovah as the name of God ever since.

In the New Testament, the translators substituted the Greek word *Kyrios* meaning Lord in place of YHWH, following the practice of the *Septuagint*.

God's Real Name

But what really is God's name? The Hebrew consonants used to spell His name are יהוה . These letters are known as the Tetragrammaton. Remember that in Hebrew, we read from right to left. As we would read them, they would be YHWH.

The true pronunciation of God's name depends upon using the proper vowels with the four consonants YHWH. What are these vowels and how sure can we be of them? Professor Anson F. Rainey of Tel Aviv University in Israel cites evidence that the pronunciation of God's name as *Yahweh* is correct. Dr. Rainey states that there are Greek transcriptions from religious papyri in Egypt which confirm this. In addition, many personal names in biblical Hebrew ending in *yahu*, which is the typical "short form" for verbs in which the last two consonants were originally *waw* (w) and *yod* (y).[1]

The evidence indicates that what we have assumed to be God's name, Jehovah, is not correct, although I doubt that He minds us calling Him by that name.

But His name is really *Yahweh*.

What Did Mary Call Jesus?

Because the New Testament was written in Greek, we have been accustomed to using the Greek forms of names. To us, God's Son is named Jesus. But that's not what Mary, a Hebrew mother, would have called Him. Mary might have leaned out of the door of their house in Nazareth and called, "*Yeshua!* Come in for supper!" She would certainly not have called out His name in Greek, Jesus.

Mary would have called her son *Yeshua*. In Hebrew, *Yeshua* is spelled ישׁוּעַ . In the Greek of the New Testament, this is spelled Ιησους , and we translate this as Joshua, except when it pertains to the Lord, when we use the Greek form — Jesus.

The word "Christ" is actually a title and not a name. It is

derived from the Greek word Χριστος , *Christos*, which means "anointed one," and is used in place of the Hebrew word *Mashiach*, meaning Messiah. Jews who have accepted Jesus as their Messiah call Him *Yeshua HaMashiach*.

The name Jesus, or Joshua, means "Yahweh is salvation." The angel informed Joseph that he should not hesitate to marry Mary, who was expecting a child, because the child had been conceived by the Holy Ghost. The angel told Joseph what the child's name was to be. "And she shall bring forth a son, and thou shalt call his name Jesus: for he shall save his people from their sins" (Matt. 1:21).

What the angel is announcing is that this child, who is to be called *Yeshua*, will assume the act of salvation which God had heretofore reserved only for himself. Jesus would become salvation to His people. No mortal man could possibly do this — Jesus had to be more than an ordinary man in order to bring salvation — He had to be God.

Yeshua was a common Hebrew name. In order to differentiate among those who bore this name, it was customary to further identify that person by adding his father's name or the place where he was from. Jesus would normally have been known as "Jesus son of Joseph," but Joseph was not actually His father. This is why He is called "Jesus of Nazareth" in the Scriptures. In the Old Testament, Joshua was called "Joshua the son of Nun," identifying him with his father.

What would Joseph have called his wife? Our Bible tells us that her name was Mary, but this is also because the Gospels were written originally in Greek. Joseph would have called her *Miriam*, which is the Hebrew form of Mary, spelled מרים in Hebrew. The Greek spelling would be Μαρτας .

Other Biblical Names

Moses is the man whom God chose to lead the Israelites out of Egyptian bondage. Moses also is responsible for the writing of the first five books of the Bible, the Pentateuch. He was born the son of Hebrew slaves but raised by the pharaoh's daughter in the royal palace. It is not so strange then that his name is really not a Hebrew name — but an Egyptian name.

Moses comes from a very common name in Egypt which actually means boy-son. In Egyptian, this name is *Mâose*.[2] Of course this name is now common among Hebrews. In modern Hebrew it has become *Moshe*. The English equivalent would be Morris.

Joseph. This name means "may God increase." It is interesting that two men by this name were associated with Jesus, one at His birth and the other at His death. Joseph, the carpenter, had provided for the young Jesus and cared for Him in the same manner that any good Hebrew father would have. Joseph of Arimathaea gave his grave to Jesus when He was taken down from the Cross. Since the "J" is pronounced as "Y," this name would have been *Yosef* in biblical times.

John. There are two men named John who immediately come to mind in the Gospels, John the Baptist and the apostle John. The name John, *Yohanan* in Hebrew, means "God has been gracious."

John the Baptizer's birth was accompanied by a miracle. His birth had been foretold by the angel Gabriel appearing to his father, the priest Zacharias (God is renowned) while the old man was offering a sacrifice in the temple. Zacharias was rendered speechless. He regained his speech after the birth of John, and confirmed that what his wife had named the child had been given to him by the angel, Gabriel. John would be the one who went before the Messiah to proclaim His coming.

John, the son of Zebedee (the gift of God), has the unique distinction of being known as the disciple whom Jesus loved. He was the only member of the Twelve who would live to an advanced age and die a natural death. It was to John that Jesus, when He was dying on the Cross, entrusted the care of His mother. John lived well into his nineties and was respected and revered by all of the early Christian church. God had indeed been gracious to both of these men named John.

Paul. This is the Greek form of the Hebrew *Shaul*, or Saul (asked for, or demanded). The apostle Paul, who began as a persecutor of Christians, became the greatest missionary of all time. Paul was born at Tarsus and his father was a Roman citizen, a fact that Paul was proud of and which on occasion helped him greatly. He was a Pharisee both by birth and belief, for this sect believed in the hope of the resurrection of the dead. Paul was a tentmaker by trade, and earned his living while he preached so as not to be a burden on those he served.

Educated under the great Jewish teacher Gamaliel, he was probably the best-educated man of his time and certainly the best-educated Christian. A prolific writer, of the 27 books which comprise the New Testament, Paul is the author of 14 of them. His appearance was certainly not imposing. From a second century description of him, he was a man of small stature, with crooked legs, of vigorous physique, partly bald, with eyes set close together, and a nose somewhat hooked.[3]

Paul lived up to his name, for his service was not only asked for by the Lord — it was demanded on the road to Damascus. After a life of hardship, imprisonment, stoning, beating, humiliation, and much success, Paul was executed by order of Nero in Rome. He was considered by the Roman authorities as "the most dangerous man in the empire." That was quite a tribute.

Noah. His name in Hebrew was *Noe*, meaning "rest." When we hear Noah's name, the ark and the great Flood immediately come to mind. Noah was the only man that God found to be righteous in the world, and it was his line that God chose to save and be the perpetuation of mankind.

Abraham. Although his name meant "the father of a multitude," he is also called "the friend of God." In fact, the Arab name for the town of Hebron, where Abraham made his home, is called *Al Khalil* — meaning "friend of God." Again God selected one man, as He had done with Noah, for a very special purpose. From Abraham would come the people God chose to be His own and to eventually bring forth His Son into the world.

David. His name meant "beloved," but would you be surprised to hear that some scholars question whether David's name was actually David — at least in his early life? In tablets found at Mari on the Euphrates, the word *Dâvídum* was found repeatedly in them.[4] In the context in which this word was used, it meant "commander" or "general." It was not a proper name, but a title. Could it be possible that the man we know as David was actually called something else as a child? Later in life when he exhibited great ability as a military leader, was he called the *Dâvídum*, the commander, and this became his name? Since the tablets found at Mari were written almost a thousand years prior to David's time, is it just a coincidence that the name and the title are so similar?

It does seem rather strange, however, that the name "David" is mentioned in the Bible referring to only one person. It must have been quite an uncommon name in those times. Some biblical scholars have long doubted that anything in the Bible before the Babylonian exile can be established with any historical accuracy. This included claims by some that David, himself, never existed and that David and his kingdom were a "myth," invented by later writers to build up a false pride in the accomplishments of early Israel.

Now an inscription has been deciphered which was found at Tel Dan in northern Galilee near the headwaters of the Jordan river. What it contains bears witness that David was indeed king of Israel and the kingdom was an important and powerful force in the Middle East at the time the Bible tells us that it was.

In 1993, Avraham Biran and his team of archaeologists from the Nelson Glueck School of Biblical Archaeology, found an inscription in a basalt stone protruding from a wall they had uncovered. In this inscription was the reference to "the king of the House of David." The script in which this is written is Old Hebrew, the type of script used before the destruction of the first temple by Nebuchadnezzar in 586 B.C.[5]

This find, together with the deciphering of the Mesha stela, which tells of the victory by the Moabite King Mesha over the Israelites territory east of the Jordan, should dispel any doubt that the biblical account of David and his kingdom are truly based on historical fact. Again archaeology has put those who relegate the Bible to "myth" and "fiction" in their place.[6]

Isaac. The meaning of this name is very appropriate. It means "laughing one," and Sarah laughed when she was told by the Lord that she would bear a son at her advanced age. Isaac was to be the child of the covenant — not Ishmael, who had been born of Sarah's Egyptian servant, Hagar. It was Isaac who was laid on the altar by his father at God's command to be sacrificed. In this way, Isaac became a *foreshadow* of Jesus, God's only begotten Son, who was the ultimate sacrifice for the sins of the world.

Jacob. He was a man of two characters and two names. Jacob was born to Isaac and Rebekah, but he was the *second* son, Esau, his twin brother, had been born first, and would have been Isaac's heir. Jacob was both a man of guile and a man of faith, a man of weakness and of strength. He refused to give his hungry brother Esau food until he had struck a bargain to obtain the birthright of his first-born brother.

When Isaac lay close to death, Jacob put on animal skins to deceive his father into thinking he was Esau, and received his father's blessing which belonged to his brother. Yet he wrestled the angel of the Lord to a draw, and refused to release his hold until the angel blessed him.

Later in life, his name would be changed to Israel, and his sons would be the patriarchs of the 12 tribes of the nation which would be called after his new name. The name Israel means "he striveth with God." It was Jacob who led his clan into Egypt to escape the famine. He was buried in the cave of Machpelah at Hebron along with Abraham and Isaac and their wives. Rebekah's grave is still to be seen on the road outside of Bethlehem where she died giving birth to Benjamin.

Methuselah. This patriarch has the distinction of living longer than any man in recorded history, 969 years. We know very little about his life except the names of the sons he sired. His name means "it shall be sent," and when he died, the great flood began.

Melchizedek. We know almost nothing at all about this man who was the priest-king of Salem. Abraham gave him tithes when Melchizedek blessed him as he returned from battle. His name means "king of righteousness," and we are told in Hebrews 7:3 that Melchizedek had neither "father, without mother, without descent, having neither beginning of days, nor end of life; but made like unto the Son of God; abideth a priest continually." His kingdom of Salem became the city of Jerusalem. Jesus was a priest *after the order of Melchizedek*. Could He have *actually been Melchizedek*? It is a matter we can't possibly know — until we can ask Him ourselves.

Adam. This name aptly means "of the ground" or "taken out of the red earth." Adam was the first *human* son of God (Gen. 3:38). The Hebrew word for man is spelled אדם . The name of the first man, Adam, is spelled אדם . They are the same. The first man gave the human race its name. We are all

Aaron

What Is God's Real Name? What Did Mary Call Jesus? • 31

man and we are all *Adam*. It was his fall that led to sin in the world. But it was by the sacrifice of the second Adam, Jesus Christ, that we can find forgiveness for our sins. The first Adam was imperfect, the second Adam was perfection.

Aaron. The older brother of Moses was chosen by God to be the spokesman, for Moses was "slow of speech." His name is fitting, it means "enlightened." From Aaron came the line of priests — Levites — for he was of the family of Kohath, who was the second son of Levi. Aaron was the first high priest.

This holy man who played such a major part in the Exodus, also fell when he allowed himself to be talked into making the golden calf while Moses was with God on the mountain. Perhaps because of this, even though Aaron repented, God would not let him enter the Promised Land. He died and was buried on Mt. Hor in Edom.

Daniel. We all remember the story of the lion's den when Daniel's name is mentioned, and he was indeed a man of great faith, refusing to obey the Babylonian king when that meant breaking faith with God. The name Daniel means "God is my Judge," and it is a fitting name for this great prophet.

In the Book of Daniel, we see the vision that Daniel received for events far in the future from his own time. There is no doubt that Daniel wrote this book himself, for although the first six chapters are in the third person, the last six are written in the first person. Daniel's prophecy included the exact date of the coming of the Messiah, which Jesus fulfilled just as Daniel prophesied — 483 years after the event which was to begin the countdown.

Isaiah. Another of the greatest Old Testament prophets was Isaiah, which means "salvation is of the Lord." Many years before the Jews were taken captive to Babylon, Isaiah prophesied the name of the king, Cyrus, who would let them return after 70 years.

He also wrote of the temple being destroyed, which happened, and his book contains many prophecies concerning the coming of the Messiah. Isaiah, according to tradition, was executed by being sawed in half.

Your Name

Names are very important. We are identified by what we are called, our names. But what we are called is not the most important thing in our lives. What is important is whether or not our names are inscribed in the Book of Life in heaven. This fact determines where each of us will spend eternity. If you are not absolutely certain that *your* name is written in the Lamb's Book of Life, then it is imperative that you accept the sacrifice Jesus Christ made for you at Calvary and commit your life to Him.

3

Abraham's Obedience —
Suppose He Had Refused

Perhaps the greatest test of faith any man in history has ever faced was the one which God imposed on Abraham. Have you ever considered what you might have done if you were put to such a test? Honestly, I do not know what I would have done if I were faced with such a decision. But Abraham was a man of exceptional faith.

Abraham had been promised by the invisible God who had led him out of Ur of the Chaldees into a foreign land that he would be the father of a mighty nation. Yet Abraham's wife, Sarah, had been barren. In an attempt to circumvent this situation, Sarah offered her maid, Hagar, as a surrogate mother for Abraham's child. But God did not have Ishmael in mind to fulfill the promise He had made.

When Isaac was born, Abraham was 100 years old and Sarah was past 90 years. Can you imagine how much Abraham must have loved this child, this child for which he had waited a hundred years? What joy must have been in this old man's heart as he watched Isaac grow. But when the boy was still young, God spoke to Abraham again and put upon his aging shoulders the most severe test imaginable to test his faith.

"And it came to pass after these things, that God did tempt Abraham, and said unto him, Abraham: and he said, Behold, here I am. And he said, Take now thy son, thine only son Isaac, whom thou lovest, and get thee into the land of Moriah; and offer him there for a burnt offering upon one of the mountains which I will tell thee of" (Gen. 22:1-2).

What must have gone through Abraham's mind when he heard this command from God! Can you imagine the sharp stab of excruciating pain which must have pierced Abraham's heart? Might not he have wondered what sort of God this must be to demand such a thing of him? What human being could have a faith so strong that it did not, at least for a fleeting instant, waver in the face of such a challenge? Did Abraham consider, if only briefly, refusing to do what God had demanded?

The Bible does not tell us anything at all about Abraham's feelings during that night. All it says is that he obeyed. "And Abraham rose up early in the morning, and saddled his ass, and took two of his young men with him, and Isaac his son, and clave the wood for the burnt offering, and rose up, and went unto the place of which God had told him" (Gen. 22:3)

Abraham had acted immediately to carry out the instructions of his God. He did not hesitate, he did not procrastinate: he acted. But the trip to the land of Moriah took three days. What a heaviness of heart Abraham must have had as the donkey plodded slowly along through the hills and valleys until he arrived at the place where God had told him to make his sacrifice. "Then on the third day Abraham lifted up his eyes, and saw the place afar off. And Abraham said unto his young men, Abide ye here with the ass; and I and the lad will go yonder and worship, and come again to you" (Gen. 22:4-5).

The young men knew nothing of what Abraham was planning to do. Apparently he had told no one of what God had commanded him. All this time, Abraham had carried in his heart this monstrous burden of sadness and grief and had communicated it to no one. He had not asked anyone for advice, he had not sought consolation, he had not shared his awesome burden with another person. Not even Sarah knew what a monumental price God had placed upon Abraham's faith. He carried all of this alone and in silence.

Abraham and his son, Isaac, climbed the mountain on which God had chosen for the sacrifice to be made. The young boy had all the confidence in the world in his father. He trusted him implicitly. "And Abraham took the wood of the burnt offering, and laid it upon Isaac his son; and he took the fire in his hand, and a knife; and they went both of them together" (Gen. 22:6).

Just as Jesus carried the wooden cross, the implement of His sacrifice, Isaac carried the wood of the burnt offering up the mountain. And just as Jesus trusted totally in His Father, Isaac did not question what was about to happen until the final moment. "And Isaac spake unto Abraham his father, and said, My father: and he said, Here am I, my son. And he said, Behold the fire and the wood: but where is the lamb for a burnt offering? And Abraham said, My son, God will provide himself a lamb for a burnt offering: so they went both of them together" (Gen. 22:7-8).

They had reached the place where God had instructed Abraham to offer his son, his beloved son, as an offering. There Abraham built an altar from the stones. Then he took a cord and bound Isaac's hands and laid his son upon the altar. "And Abraham stretched forth his hand, and took the knife to slay his son" (Gen. 22:10).

The moment had come! Abraham raised his arm, the knife pointed down at Isaac. Can you imagine what was going through Isaac's mind as his eyes widened and he realized what his father — the father he had trusted without question — was about to do? But Abraham had already passed God's test of faith. "And the angel of the Lord called unto him out of heaven, and said, Abraham, Abraham: and he said, Here am I. And he said, Lay not thine hand upon the lad, neither do any thing unto him: for now I know that thou fearest God, seeing thou hast not withheld thy son, thine only son from me" (Gen. 22:11-12).

What if Abraham had refused?

I am certain that you have seen the parallel between Abraham's willingness to obey God, even if that meant the death of his only and beloved son, and 2,000 years later, when another Son would be the sacrifice. But if Abraham had refused to offer up Isaac, would the Father had sent His only begotten and beloved Son to die for the sins of mankind?

Mankind has free will. Each of us makes a conscious decision whether to obey God or not. Abraham could have refused to offer Isaac as a sacrifice to God. What would have been God's reaction if he had not been willing? There is a clue in what God might have done in the verses which follow. "And the angel of the Lord called unto Abraham out of heaven the second time, And said, By myself have I sworn, saith the Lord, for because thou hast done this thing, and hast not withheld thy son, thine only son: That in blessing I will bless thee, and in multiplying I will multiply thy seed as the stars of the heaven, and as the sand which is upon the sea shore; and thy seed shall possess the gate of his enemies; And in thy seed shall all the nations of the earth be blessed; because thou hast obeyed my voice" (Gen. 22: 15-18).

Because Abraham had proven himself willing not to withhold even his son from God, God made the covenant with Abraham that not only would his descendants be as numerous as the stars of heaven and the sand of the shore, but that from Abraham's seed would come the One who would be a blessing to all nations of the earth. And because a mere man, Abraham, was willing to offer his only son to God as a sacrifice, God was therefore willing to offer His only Son to be the redemptive sacrifice for all of mankind's sins.

There are those who say that all of this was planned from the beginning, that Jesus was to be the sacrificial lamb from the foundations of the earth. This may be true, but from whose seed Jesus was to come had perhaps not been decided. It was Abraham's obedience that allowed God to make that decision.

It was Abraham's obedience which made his seed the chosen people, selected to bring God's only begotten Son into the world to die so that mankind could be reconciled to their Creator. If Abraham had refused, God would have had to find another man — and another people — to be the line of humanity from which He would bring forth His Son into the world. But what would happen about 500 years later, almost made God change His mind.

Isaac's son, Jacob, was to bring his family into Egypt to escape a famine in Canaan. After the pharaoh that Joseph served died, the Hebrews were made slaves. Four hundred and thirty years later, another descendant of Abraham was to be the instrument of God to bring them out of Egypt and prepare them for the inheritance which God had promised to Abraham's seed.

Moses had gone up on Mount Sinai to receive the Ten Commandments from the hand of God. But when Moses delayed in returning to the Israelites who waited below, they thought that he had died on the mountain. Without Moses as their leader, they were afraid. They convinced Aaron to make them an idol, a golden calf from their earrings. And they worshipped it and sacrificed to it. "... and they said, These be thy gods, O Israel, which brought thee up out of the land of Egypt" (Exod. 32:4).

And God's wrath was stirred as He saw what they had done. Although He had promised to make the seed of Abraham into a great nation, now God had second thoughts about what He had promised. "And the Lord said unto Moses, I have seen this people, and, behold, it is a stiffnecked people: Now therefore let me alone, that my wrath may wax hot against them, and that I may consume them: and I will make of thee a great nation" (Exod. 32:9-10).

God was ready to completely destroy the Israelites. What He offered to Moses was to cancel His promise to Abraham and transfer this promise to Moses. Perhaps any man but Moses would have readily accepted God's offer. But Moses was another exceptional man. "And Moses besought the Lord his God, and said, Lord, why doth thy wrath wax hot against thy people, which thou hast brought forth out of the land of Egypt with great power, and with a mighty hand? Wherefore should the Egyptians speak, and say, For mischief did he bring them out, to slay them in the mountains, and to consume them from the face of the earth? Turn from thy fierce wrath, and repent of the evil against thy people" (Exod. 32:11-12).

Moses then reminded God that He had sworn by His own self to Abraham, Isaac, and Jacob that He would multiply their seed and give them the land of Canaan as an inheritance forever. Moses reminded God that if He destroyed the Israelites, that act would reduce His stature in the eyes of the Egyptians, the people to whom God had just demonstrated His might and power. Moses refused to accept the greatest gift that God could bestow upon any man — being the father of the chosen people of the Lord. Instead, he was more concerned about how the pagan people would view this invisible God of the Hebrews. "And the Lord repented of the evil which he thought to do unto his people" (Exod. 32:14).

But this generation of Israelites would not be allowed to

enter the land of their inheritance. After they had shown reluctance to depend on God to fight their battles against the people of Canaan and their fear of entering that land after most of the spies gave a bad report, God made them wander for 40 additional years in the wilderness. All of those who had left the captivity of Egypt, except for Joshua and Caleb, died during their wandering. Not even Moses was allowed to go into the land that God had promised to the descendants of Abraham.

But then, almost 700 years later, God's anger was again raised against His people. Solomon's sons had divided the kingdom into the northern part, Israel, and the southern part, Judah. Israel forgot God and this time there was no Moses to plead for them. God raised up the Assyrians and the 10 tribes of the northern kingdom were obliterated. This left only the tribes of Judah and Benjamin.

But these people also forgot the Lord, and God raised up the Babylonians to punish them. The remnant of those who had come out of Egypt were again subjected to imprisonment as God allowed them to remain captive in Babylon for 70 years before restoring them to their promised land.

At last, in the fullness of God's time, His only begotten Son entered the world to fulfill His mission to be the final and ultimate sacrifice for the redemption of mankind. But one cannot help wonder how things might have been different had Abraham refused to offer Isaac to the Lord as he had been commanded. And in Abraham's obedience in not withholding his only son, how God, himself, would not do otherwise with His beloved and only begotten Son.

4

Whatever Happened to Pontius Pilate?

One of the most famous — and infamous — men in history was the Roman procurator of Judea, Pontius Pilate. It was by this man's order that Jesus was allowed to be executed. The Bible mentions Pontius Pilate only in relation to the trial of Jesus.

But who was this man? How did he gain the position of procurator of Judea? And what happened to him later?

Let us see what we can find out about this sinister and enigmatic character who played such a major and pivotal part in the most important event in Christianity — the crucifixion and resurrection of Jesus of Nazareth.

What we know of Pontius Pilate comes primarily from the Gospels, from what the Jewish historian Josephus wrote about his governorship of Judea, and from an incident related by Philo. Tacitus also mentions Pontius Pilate in reference to the "execution of Christus" in his *Annals of Imperial Rome.* A stone slab has been found at Caesarea engraved with the names of Tiberius and Pontius Pilate. The inscription is incomplete, giving only two known names but omitting his first name. However, it is firm archaeological evidence that Pontius Pilate was indeed procurator of Judea.

His family name, Pontius, was rather common throughout central and northern Italy at all levels of society. Men from that family were consuls of Rome in A.D. 17 and in A.D. 37. His cognomen *Pilatus* is interesting in itself. This is an extremely rare name and has a fascinating meaning — "armed with a javelin." Since a spear was thrust through the side of Jesus to ascertain His death, and a javelin is a form of spear, the name of the man who ordered the execution of Jesus was quite appropriate.[1]

Pontius Pilate would have been a member of an equestrian class of Roman society, similar to the social position held by a knight in medieval times. He was above the middle class but definitely not of aristocratic stock. In all probability, he came from a military family and served as a military or administrative tribune with a Roman legion before his elevation to procurator of Judea.

Pilate's wife, Claudia Procula, was a woman of equal or slightly higher social status.[2] It may have been through her family's influence that Pilate met the man who was to be his mentor, a man who was at one time even more powerful and feared than the emperor Tiberius. This was Lucius Aelius Sejanus, prefect of the praetorian guard, and the man the emperor referred to as the "partner of my labors."

Sejanus was absolutely ruthless, and he attracted men of similar morality, finding positions for them in the administration of the empire where they would be useful in accomplishing his goal of becoming emperor of Rome himself. Sejanus had been Tiberius' confidant and "hatchet man" for many years before Tiberius became emperor. In fact, it was Sejanus who was responsible for the deaths of those who were ahead of Tiberius in line to succeed Augustus Caesar.

When Tiberius became emperor, Sejanus was made commander of the praetorian guard, the soldiers who were responsible for protecting the life of the man who ruled the empire. In that capacity, Sejanus continued to kill the enemies of Tiberius, including the emperor's own children and grandchildren who were thought to be rivals to power.

Tiberius was a suspicious and paranoid man, and the emperor's fears were continually reinforced by Sejanus until Tiberius trusted no one except the commander of his personal guard. Eventually no one could gain access to Tiberius unless the appointment was arranged by Lucius Sejanus. The men appointed to military and political positions were usually those who had the backing of the commander of the guard.

In time, Sejanus was not satisfied with merely being the

most powerful man in the Roman empire. He also desired the
title and royal trappings of the office of emperor. His plan
was to have Tiberius name him as his successor in his will,
then to assassinate the unsuspecting emperor.

To accomplish this, Sejanus must have his own loyal men
in the high positions of the empire. You can imagine the type
of person that Sejanus wished to have in these positions.
Pontius Pilate was one of these men, loyal to Lucius Sejanus,
and of the same character as his mentor: ruthless, ambitious,
and totally devoid of ethics and morality.[3]

Pontius Pilate — Procurator of Judea

In A.D. 26, Pilate was appointed procurator of Judea to
replace Valerius Gratus. It is evident from the beginning of
his administration that he shared Lucius Sejanus' hatred and
contempt of the Jews. Nor did he understand the religious
temperament of the people he was to govern. Judea was a
minor province and although Pilate would be responsible for
the civil and judicial administration, he would be subordi-
nate to the general authority of the Roman legate of Syria, the
supreme military commander in the East, in any military
matters.

Pilate, as procurator, commanded the Roman garrison in
Judea consisting of a squadron of cavalry (120 men) and four
or five cohorts of infantry (2,500 to 3,000 men). The troops
were stationed primarily in Caesarea, Pilate's headquarters,
with a cohort of infantry at Sabaste and a small garrison at the
fortress of Antonia in Jerusalem. On feast days, when the
population of Jerusalem would swell to over a million Jews,
the troops in Jerusalem were heavily reinforced with the
troops from Caesarea to prevent disturbances.

His first offense against the Jews was to allow his soldiers to keep the pagan images on their standards as they
marched into Jerusalem, something which his predecessors
had been careful to remove. These images were worshipped
by the Roman soldiers and were considered idolatrous to the
Jews. There was a protest against this blasphemy and a
delegation of Jewish leaders demanded an audience with the
procurator. Pilate threatened these men with instant death if
they did not go away, but this did not sway the delegation.

After a five-day standoff, Pilate was forced to give in to

their demand to remove the offensive images from the standards. But his pride had suffered a blow and he retaliated. When he was in residence in Jerusalem, Pilate occupied Herod the Great's old palace. He had gold shields brought in from Caesarea which bore the inscription of Tiberius engraved on them and hung these on the walls of the palace in Jerusalem.

Again there was a protest from the Jews, who saw this as an attempt to introduce emperor-worship into Judea. This was already flourishing elsewhere in the empire, with temples constructed where sacrifices were made to Caesar. It took a delegation of Jews who journeyed to Rome to personally see Tiberius in order to have these offensive emblems removed from Jerusalem. Pilate had the shields removed and placed in the temple dedicated to Augustus Caesar at Caesarea.

These first two confrontations ended without bloodshed. The next would not. It is ironic that this was caused by Pilate attempting to improve the quality of life in Jerusalem, which suffered greatly from a lack of water during the population increase on feast days. Pilate decided to construct an aqueduct to bring water to the city from a spring about 25 miles away.

Pilate had no money for such a project. He reasoned that since this was for the betterment of the Jewish population of Jerusalem, they should pay for it. There was substantial money in the temple treasury. Pilate used this sacred money, called the corban, from the temple to pay the cost of construction for the aqueduct.

Tens of thousands of Jews arose in protest against this project. The procurator was aware that only two things were expected of him by Rome: prompt payment of Roman taxes by the Jews and to allow no civil uprising against the authority of Rome. He sent his troops into the crowd of demonstrators in disguise. Each soldier carried a club hidden beneath his robe.

On command, the soldiers produced their clubs and quelled the riot, but many Jews were beaten to death. This may have been the incident which Jesus mentioned in Luke 13:1 when He referred to the Galileans whose blood Pilate had mingled with their sacrifices. It was probably this incident also which caused the enmity between Pilate and Herod

Antipas, for if Galileans were killed they would have been subjects of Herod Antipas.

For the first five years of Pilate's administration, he had no real concern about his treatment of the Jews. Lucius Sejanus was his mentor and protector in Rome and he had no fear of Tiberius, even if delegations were sent to complain about his actions. But events were taking place in Rome which would drastically alter the security of his position.

Lucius Sejanus' ambition would no longer wait to be fulfilled and he decided to act. Tiberius had made him a consul of Rome but even this did not satisfy his growing lust for power. He seduced Livilla, the wife of Tiberius' son Drusus who was the heir apparent to succeed his father as emperor. Then Sejanus arranged to have Drusus poisoned. After a proper time of waiting, he approached Tiberius and asked for Livilla's hand in marriage, which would have raised his social status into the Roman aristocracy. He also requested that Tiberius adopt him as a son.

However, by this time Tiberius was beginning to suspect that the man who was charged with protecting his life was conspiring against him. When Sejanus' divorced wife came to him with the charge that it had been her former husband who had poisoned Drusus, the emperor had Sejanus arrested and executed. Pontius Pilate was now without his mentor and protector. His actions would be judged solely by Tiberius and he was forced to placate his Jewish subjects, especially the priests and religious leaders.

The Trial of Jesus

Just before Passover in A.D. 33, a man was brought before him by the priests and accused of crimes worthy of death. This was necessary because only the Roman procurator could sentence a man to be executed in Judea. Because Passover would begin at sundown, the man's accusers could not enter the Roman hall. To do so would have rendered them "unclean" by entering a building which was polluted by leaven, and they would not be able to celebrate the Passover feast. Pilate had to come out onto the pavement in front of the *praetorium*, which was a part of the Antonia fortress, to hear their charges against this man.

Their first charge was simply that this man, Jesus of

Nazareth, was an "evildoer" (John 18:28-32). Pilate smirked at this, telling them that if that was all the man was accused of, they should take him away and punish him according to their own laws. Their reply was that they were not allowed to sentence a man to death, only Pilate could do that.

It was clear to the priests that more serious charges would have to be presented. They then charged that Jesus was perverting the nation, forbidding the people to pay their taxes to Caesar, and calling himself Christ the King. This was a more serious charge and Pilate would have to consider it.

He brought Jesus into the hall, leaving his accusers outside, and questioned him. Pilate asked Jesus whether he was indeed the King of the Jews. All Jesus would reply was, "Thou sayest that."

We must remember that Pilate was a Roman, and although he was not in any respect a religious man, he was used to Roman gods. The charge of calling himself Christ meant that he was the Son of God. In Roman religion, gods often were known to assume the form of a man and walk the earth. When questioned about where His kingship was located, Jesus replied that it was not of this world.

Satisfied that the man claimed only a "philosophical kingship," an idea familiar to him from the Stoics, he questioned Jesus further, asking him "What is truth?"

Pilate left the hall and confronted the priests, waiting outside. "I find in him no fault at all," he told them.

They were outraged. Pilate probably enjoyed this, for in spite of having to deal with the Jewish leaders, he still despised them. But then Pilate learned that Jesus was from Galilee. Herod Antipas was in Jerusalem. Pilate had found a way in which he could accomplish two things; get these Jewish religious leaders off his back, and also do something which might mend fences with the tetrarch of Galilee. He decided to send Jesus to Herod Antipas for judgment.

Pilate was correct in one aspect of this — Antipas was flattered that he had sent Jesus to him. He had heard about the Galilean who performed miracles, and he was anxious to meet him. Perhaps this strange man would perform a miracle right before his eyes. But the tetrarch was disappointed. He sent Jesus back to Pilate.

Again the procurator of Judea came out and sat in the

seat of judgment. His wife, Claudia Procula, came out to him and whispered in her husband's ear, ". . . Have thou nothing to do with that just man: for I have suffered many things this day in a dream because of him" (Matt. 27:19).

Pilate made another attempt to save Jesus from His accusers. He offered them a choice between releasing Jesus and releasing some other prisoner, which was a custom at Passover to do. The crowd, urged on by the priests, rejected the release of Jesus, shouting, "Release Barabbas!"

There was another shout, one which Pilate could not ignore. "We have no king but Caesar!" (John 19:15). "If you let this man go, thou art not Caesar's friend!" (John 19:12).

In his heart Pilate knew that Jesus had done nothing to deserve the sentence of death. He had broken no Roman law. Jesus should be released no matter what the priests demanded. But Pilate was in a delicate position, no longer protected by his mentor in Rome. If he set this man free, the Jews would accuse him of abetting treason. "What shall I do then with Jesus which is called Christ?" he asked the crowd.

The response came back: "Crucify him!" (Matt. 27:22).

Pilate was more interested in his own welfare than in justice. He called for a basin of water and washed his hands, signifying that his own hands would be clean of the execution of a innocent man. "I am innocent of the blood of this just person," Pilate told them, "see ye to it" (Matt. 27:24).

Again there was a shout from the crowd. "His blood be on us, and on our children" (Matt. 27:25).

Pilate motioned to his soldiers. They took Jesus into the hall where He was scourged, mocked, and forced to carry the heavy cross-bar though the streets of Jerusalem on the way to Golgotha. And there Jesus was executed. There is much more to say, for what happened after that is the most important event in history. Neither death nor the tomb were capable of holding the Son of God. Three days later was His glorious resurrection. But we are concerned here only with Pontius Pilate.

What Happened to Pontius Pilate?

The Bible is silent regarding what happened to Pontius Pilate. According to Josephus, his political career came to an end six years later. A Samaritan announced that he knew where Moses had hidden the holy vessels from the taber-nacle. He told his countrymen that if they would accompany him to Mt. Gerizim, he would show them where these sacred objects had been buried.

Ignoring the fact that Moses had never crossed over the Jordan River, nor set foot in Samaria, the man's claim was received by many people with great joy and enthusiasm.

Crowds of people swarmed to the mountain and a fervor began to build among them. A rumor was circulated that when these holy things were unearthed, God would deliver His people from oppression and they would regain their status as a great nation. Pilate heard of this and acted quickly.

A detachment of Roman soldiers was dispatched imme-diately to the village of Tirathaba at the foot of Mt. Gerizim, and prepared to climb the mountain and unearth the vessels. When Pilate's soldiers arrived, they saw that the crowd also carried weapons. They blocked the roads leading from the village and attacked the crowd. Many of the Samaritans were killed, most of them fled, and the rest were taken prisoner and later executed.

A delegation was sent to Vitellis, the Roman governor of Syria, accusing Pontius Pilate of the murder of peaceful Samaritans who were not in revolt against Rome, but merely looking for buried sacred objects. Vitellis, long aware of Pilate's vicious attitude and actions, sent one of his subordi-nates named Marcellus to take charge of the affairs of Judea and ordered Pilate to Rome to answer to these accusations before the emperor. Pilate had no choice but to sail to Rome, but during the voyage Tiberius Caesar died.[4]

Gaius Caesar, known better as Caligula, became em-peror of Rome. Pilate would have certainly presented his case before the new emperor, but there are no records available as to this. Eusebius, almost 300 years later, states that Pilate was caught up in calamity and was forced to become his own executioner and to "punish himself with his own hand." Eusebius remarks that "divine justice, it seems, was not slow to overtake him."[5]

But other traditions and legends somewhat recount stories about what happened to Pontius Pilate and his wife, Claudia Procula. One of these states that he was banished to Vienne on the Rhone river in the south of France, while another claims that he sought solitude from Roman politics on the mountain near Lake Lucerne now known as Mt. Pilatus. This legend has it that after years of depression over what he had done, he leaped from a precipice into the lake and was drowned.[6]

A similar story concerning Pilate states that he retired to a village on the slopes of Mt. Vesuvius where he drank heavily, either from depression caused by his failed political career or from a convicting conscience over his part in the crucifixion of Jesus. In any event, this account states that both he and his wife were killed by the eruption of the volcano in A.D. 79.

But there is another tradition that tells something quite different about Pontius Pilate and his wife, Claudia Procula, and this appears to have a bit more substantiation than the others from early Christian writers. In this account, Pontius Pilate and his wife were both put to death as Christian martyrs.[7]

Turtullian (A.D. 155-245) called Pilate a "Christian by conscience" in his book *Apologeticus,* and also attributed a letter from Pilate which commended the Christian faith. Origen (A.D. 185-254) described Claudia Procula, Pilate's wife, as a convert to Christianity.[8] There is an apocryphal *Acts of Pilate* in existence today which was first mentioned by Epiphanius (A.D. 315-403) in which Pilate's actions after the Resurrection are noted.

On the basis of this legend, both Pontius Pilate and his wife are venerated as saints in the Ethiopian church. Their feast day is celebrated each year on June 25. The Greek church honors only Claudia Procula as a saint with a feast day on October 27.

There is no doubt that Pilate's wife had some type of emotional experience in the form of a dream (Matt. 27:19). It is not clear, however, whether this was from God or Satan. Peter, immediately after he had proclaimed Jesus to be the Son of God, had been influenced by the devil to attempt to prevent Jesus from going to Jerusalem where He would be crucified. Jesus rebuked Peter, saying, "Get thee behind me, Satan . . ." (Matt. 16:23). It is possible that Satan was using Pilate's wife to attempt to circumvent the Crucifixion and Resurrection, just as he had tried to use Peter.

We cannot be certain whether Claudia Procula's dream was from God or the devil. But Pilate's wife may indeed have become a Christian. Certainly she became aware of the account of the Resurrection, for it was circulated widely both immediately after He arose and by His disciples later. If her dream was vivid enough to compel her to come to her husband with a warning not to harm Jesus, the startling message of His resurrection would have had a dramatic and profound effect upon her. It is no stretch of the imagination to think that this experience would lead to her conversion to Christianity.

The New Testament writers are not hostile toward Pilate. Perhaps they understood that it was completely in the will of God that Jesus be sentenced to death. Certainly, without the Crucifixion there could have been no Resurrection. This attitude is reflected by later Christian writers, and Pilate was even described as "blessed," for in his governorship "all was fulfilled."[9]

Nor should Pilate's conversion be considered impossible. He was not the first man who began as a persecutor of Jesus and became a devout follower. The apostle Paul is sufficient proof of that. And if Pilate, the man who was at least indirectly responsible for the death of Jesus Christ, may find forgiveness for his act then is this not a wonderful message to us all: that with genuine and heartfelt repentance, there is no sin too great to be forgiven.

Pontius Pilate asked of our Lord, "What is truth?"

Perhaps, just perhaps, even he was able to find it!

5

The Tower of Babel — What Was the Original Language?

The Bible tells us that at one time the whole world spoke just one language. If the biblical account of the great flood of Noah is correct, and all life except Noah's family was destroyed, then this would have been an obvious result. Certainly Noah's three sons all spoke the same language, and their descendants also would have spoken that tongue. "And the whole earth was of one language, and of one speech" (Gen. 11:1).

But today, there are approximately 5,000 languages in the world. What happened? What was the original language spoken by Noah and his sons? The Bible tells us what happened. The sons of Noah and their families journeyed to the east and found a suitable place to build a city on the plain called Shinar.

There was an abundance of clay with which to make bricks and there was petroleum oozing from the ground. This was the "slime," or asphalt which they could use as mortar in construction. But the people decided to build more than just a city, they planned to construct something else. "And they said, Go to, let us build us a city and a tower, whose top may reach unto heaven; and let us make a name, lest we be scattered abroad upon the face of the whole earth" (Gen. 11:4).

The Lord saw what they were doing and came down for a closer look. What God saw, greatly disturbed Him. "And the Lord said, Behold, the people is one, and they have all one language; and this they begin to do: and now nothing will be restrained from them, which they have imagined to do. . . . let us go down, and there confound their language, that they may not understand one another's speech" (Gen. 11:6-7)

Here we see that it was God who caused the proliferation of languages. And it was from one geographical point that these languages spread, when the inhabitants of that city scattered across the face of the earth. "So the Lord scattered them abroad from thence upon the face of all the earth: and they left off to build the city. Therefore is the name of it called Babel; because the Lord did there confound the language of all the earth: and from thence did the Lord scatter them abroad upon the face of all the earth" (Gen. 11:8-9).

Is there any scientific evidence that supports the Genesis account of this tower, and that all the languages of the world originated here? Have archaeologists found traces of such a building? What light can modern linguists throw on such a dispersion of people, each group carrying with it a different tongue? Let's look at the evidence and see for ourselves.

The Tower of Babel

The name Babel itself comes from the Hebrew word *Babel*, meaning "gate of god." A similar Hebrew root, *balal*, means "confusion" or "mixing."[1] From "Babel" the name of the surrounding country was derived, the nation we know as Babylonia. Hence, it is linguistic confirmation that the name given in the Genesis account for this place, Babel, was actually the name by which the native people knew it.

The Genesis account states that the families of the sons of Noah found a valley, called Shinar. They had come from where the ark had landed on Mt. Ararat to find this plain. Archaeologists have found evidence that something exactly like that happened. The Reader's Digest *Atlas of the Bible* states, "Then about 3500 B.C. a non-Semitic people called the Sumerians, who are generally believed to have originated in central Asia, arrived on the scene. Genesis 11:2 preserves what may be a reference to the coming of the Sumerians: 'And as men migrated from the east, they found a plain in the land of Shinar (Sumer) and settled there.' "

The remains of many "towers," *migdol* in Hebrew, have been found by archaeologists in what is now Iraq. Also found was the text of an inscription by Sharkalisharri, king of Agade in about 2250 B.C., mentioning his restoration of the temple-tower (ziggurat) at Babylon. This implies the existence of a previous sacred city on the site.

After Sharkalisharri restored the ziggurat, it was apparently destroyed again. There are records of its restoration again by Esarhaddon in 681-665 B.C. Its name in Sumerian was Etemenanki, meaning "the Building of the Foundation-platform of Heaven and Earth." This was associated with the temple of the Babylonian god Marduk Esagila, "the building whose top is in heaven."[2]

Very probably the construction of this ziggurat and temple followed an earlier plan of the one which had been destroyed. Again, this confirms what we are told in Genesis; that the people wished to build a tower to reach heaven. The subsequent ziggurats with their temples placed at the highest portion of the series of platforms followed the plan of the original construction of the sons of Noah, whose efforts had been thwarted by God's intervention.

This ziggurat was severely damaged in war (652-648 B.C.), but was rebuilt by Nebuchadnezzar II (605-562 B.C.). Herodotus visited this site in 460 B.C. and described it. "The temple is a square building, two furlongs each way, with bronze gates, and was still in existence in my time; it has a solid central tower, one furlong square, with a second erected on top of it and then a third, and so on up to eight. All eight towers can be climbed by a spiral way running round the outside, and about halfway up there are seats for those who make the ascent to rest on. On the summit of the topmost tower stands a great temple with a fine large couch in it, richly covered, and a golden table beside it. The shrine contains no image and no one spends the night there except (if we may believe the Chaldeans who are the priests of Bel) one Assyrian woman, all alone, whoever it may be that the god has chosen. The Chaldeans say — though I do not believe them — that the god enters the temple in person and takes his rest upon the bed."[3]

Part of this building was unearthed in 1899 and the dimensions given by Herodotus and in a cuneiform tablet dated 229 B.C. were checked. The foundation stage was found to be 295 by 295 feet and was 108 feet in height. Above this were built the other platforms, each 20 to 60 feet in height, with diminishing area.[4] The top platform was crowned with a temple and access to the summit was by stairway or ramp.

The vitrified remains of a ziggurat were found at Borsippa (Birs Nimrud) in Iraq, just seven miles from the city of Baghdad. The government of Iraq, under Sadam Hussein, is restoring this ziggurat as a symbol of the neo-Babylonian fervor of the present government.

There can be no doubt of the truth of the biblical account in Genesis concerning a city and tower being constructed on the plain of Shinar. There is considerable archaeological evidence to substantiate what the Bible tells us. But what about the confusion of tongues? Is there any proof that it was God who created the languages spoken throughout the world today when He stopped the construction of the tower of Babel? Let's look at what science can tell us about that.

The Origin of Languages

The Bible tells us that God confused the languages of those who were building the tower of Babel and scattered them over the face of the earth. What does science tell us about the diversity of language and how these were taken to various parts of the earth?

In the November 5, 1990, edition of *U. S. News & World Report* there was an article titled "The Mother Tongue." In this article was presented the latest findings of linguists who are working backward from modern speech in an attempt to find and re-create the first language used by the human race.

This article begins by relating a discovery made in 1786 by Sir William Jones, an Englishman serving as a judge in India. An Oriental scholar, Jones was learning Sanskrit, the language in which many ancient Indian religious and literary texts are written. He found, to his amazement, that Sanskrit's grammar and vocabulary bore a remarkable resemblance to those of Greek and Latin. It was evident that all three languages had sprung from a common source.

But Greek and Latin were European languages while Sanskrit was an ancient tongue used many thousands of miles from Europe in India. How could these languages possibly have a common source?

Linguists of today, using the most advanced techniques possible, are still trying to find the answer to this question. There are over 5,000 languages spoken in the world. Could all of these have arisen from one prime language spoken thousands of years back in time?

They have not found this ancient tongue, but they have made some startling discoveries. Linguists have developed a "language tree," with the various branches representing families of languages. The trunk of this tree seems to be what is called "Proto-Indo-European." From this trunk branch the base languages which have been developed from Proto-Indo-European over the years.

But where did this "trunk" language originate? Soviet scholars like Gamkrelidze Ivanov cite words in proto-Indo-European that appear to have been borrowed from the languages of Mesopotamia and the Near East. This suggests that the original speakers of proto-Indo-European at one time lived in close proximity to people who spoke the languages of Mesopotamia.

For example, the word for wine appears to have its roots in the Semitic word *wanju* and the Egyptian word *wns*. When the English word, *eat*, is compared to words meaning the same thing around the world, we trace the following lineage:

Proto-World	Hita
Amerind	Hit-
Nostraic	-ita
Indo-European	Hed
Greek	Edmenai
Latin	Edere
Old German	Ezzan
English	Eat

If these languages were taken around the world by those people that God scattered from Mesopotamia, then there should also be other avenues of scientific investigation to show that this indeed happened. Genetics has already shown that the first man (Adam) and the first woman (Eve) lived where the Bible tells us that the Garden of Eden was located.[5] Can the science of genetics tell us anything about the spread of languages around the world?

As a matter of fact, it can — and does! Comparing genes from people around the world, biologists have created a family tree for humanity. The human race can be divided into seven major groups, each the result of ancient migrations. But the interesting fact is, these seven major groups roughly mirror the major language families which have been reconstructed by linguists.[6]

This means that both the sciences, linguistics and genetics, agree that at one time all people spoke a single language and were in the same geographic area. Something caused these people to separate, and as they did they took with them both their genetic identification — and language. Isn't this exactly what we are told in Genesis?

But if these people in Mesopotamia all spoke the same language, what was this original language that they spoke? The linguistic experts are attempting to find the root language from which the seven major language groups evolved. But their research has thus far not been very fruitful. For the Bible believer, this should not be surprising. God has given us the answer in Genesis when He confused their tongues and each workman on the tower of Babel spoke a new and different language.

But the linguistic scholars have provided us with some extremely interesting data. The "language tree" they have drawn, with all of its branches and shoots representing how each language developed from a parent branch, reveals an interesting bit of information. Nowhere on this tree do we find the language in which the Old Testament was written — the language in which God spoke to all generations to come. Nowhere on the branches of this complex "language tree" do we find Hebrew!

Nor should we expect to find it. It has been shown that Adam wrote down on clay tablets what God told him happened before Adam was created.[7] Subsequent patriarchs recorded the history of their times in a like manner. When Moses wrote the Book of Genesis, he had in front of him the written history from Adam to Joseph, written in the language of Hebrew, of course. The original language was Hebrew.

Linguistic experts can use the most advanced methods of analysis, utilize the most powerful computers available, and they will probably never come up with the right answer to this quest for the "mother tongue." But the Bible believer needs no such equipment. God has given us the answer, and it was written down long ago in the first of all languages.

It was written in Hebrew.

6

Biblical Symbolism

The books of both the Old and New Testaments are rich in symbolism, with such things as rocks, candlesticks, oil, serpents, and even the rainbow after a thunderstorm having meaning. It would take an entire book to enumerate all of the symbolism in the Bible. In this short chapter, we will touch on only a few.

Some of these symbols are obvious, some are not so obvious. We can understand immediately that the serpent in the Garden of Eden is Satan, and can recognize at once that this is the personification of all that is evil in the world. But do we also realize that the words spoken to Eve by this serpent, "Ye shall not surely die," is symbolic of man's questioning the Word of God, and his rebellion against God's laws? All sin begins when we question the rules which the Creator, for our own good, has placed upon mankind.

Noah's Ark

Noah's ark was not only the boat which carried Noah and his family to safety during the Flood, it was also a symbol of what was to come. Just as the Lord gave Noah the detailed instructions of how this ship was to be constructed, God gives each of us the plans for our own personal ark of safety. Jesus Christ is our only ark of safety in this life and for the eternity to come. The ark which carried the seed of humanity through destruction in Noah's time was a foreshadow, a symbol of Jesus Christ.

The rainbow which appeared in the sky after the Flood was a symbol of God's promise to mankind that He would never again destroy the entire world with water. This certainly did not mean that there would be no local floods, but the Lord would not use another worldwide flood to wipe humanity from the earth. The use of a bow as a symbol also has a deeper meaning. "I do set my bow in the cloud, and it shall be for a token of a covenant between me and the earth" (Gen. 9:13).

When God set His bow in the cloud, it was unstrung. In effect, God had unilaterally disarmed himself. The Lord had declared a truce between himself and man. When Noah had built an altar and burned a sacrifice to God after they had come safely through the Flood, God had made this vow: ". . . I will not again curse the ground any more for man's sake; for the imagination of man's heart is evil from his youth; neither will I again smite any more every thing living, as I have done" (Gen. 8:21).

The curse which God had placed on the ground after Adam's fall, He lifted after Noah's obedience, not for Noah's sake alone but because God knew that man, in himself, was incapable of righteousness. Mankind needed a Saviour, another ark of safety.

Abraham

The Book of Genesis gives us a detailed account of the life of Abraham. Not only was this man a "friend of God," as James 2:23 tells us, but his life was full of symbolism. Abraham was a man who "believed God," he trusted in what God told him, and his faith was unshakable. And in the life of this man who was to become the father of the nation from which God would bring forth the Saviour, there are two events which are symbolic of the birth and crucifixion of Jesus Christ.

Although he had been promised by God that his seed would be as numerous as the grains of sand of the sea, Abraham's wife remained barren. Sarah was over 90 years of age, well past any hope of having a child, and Abraham was 100 years of age. But still Abraham clung to God's promise and believed that God would fulfill His promise. "And the Lord visited Sarah as he had said, and the Lord did unto Sarah as he had spoken. For Sarah conceived, and bare Abraham a son in his old age, at the set time of which God had spoken to him" (Gen. 21:1-2).

There was no way that Sarah could have conceived and borne a child at her advanced age. Her female reproductive organs had degenerated into uselessness. It was only by an act of God that these were regenerated. This Scripture tells us that the Lord visited her, and the Holy Spirit performed a miracle. Sarah conceived.

This, I believe, is a symbolic representation of something which was to occur 2,000 years later when a virgin was to conceive and bear a child. What God was showing to those who doubt that this could happen, is that with Him anything is possible. Certainly, if God could regenerate the reproductive organs of a 90-year-old woman who had never borne a child, then He is also capable of causing a virgin to conceive. The birth of Isaac was, I am convinced, a symbolic foreshadow of the virgin birth.

Isaac was the only son, the beloved son, of Abraham. When the Lord then commanded Abraham to take his son to a mountain and offer him as a burnt offering, this is also a symbol. For just as Abraham was willing to give Isaac's life as a sacrifice, God was also willing to give His beloved, His only begotten Son, as a sacrifice.

Abraham was said to have believed God, and his faith was imputed to him as righteousness. Isaac did not question what his father was about to do when he was bound and placed on the altar. Jesus also trusted in His Father, and was obedient even to death to His Heavenly Father's will. In that obedience and in that sacrifice, we all have the promise of eternal life.

Egypt

Egypt! How that name conjures up thoughts of great monuments, the pyramids, the Sphinx, the splendor of the pharaohs. But Egypt is also symbolic of something else. God uses Egypt to signify sin.

When the 70 Hebrews entered Egypt to escape the famine, the nation that was to be forged from their descendants had symbolically entered into sin.

Four hundred years later, as a result of divine intervention, they were to leave Egypt for a Promised Land. On the night of the Exodus, they were instructed to slay a lamb and to place this lamb's blood on the doorposts of their houses.

"And the blood shall be to you a token upon the houses where ye are: and when I see the blood, I will pass over you, and the plague shall not be upon you to destroy you, when I smite the land of Egypt" (Exod. 12:13).

The blood of the Passover lamb was a symbol of the blood shed by the ultimate Passover Lamb. When the Lamb of God, His only begotten and beloved Son, shed His blood on the cross, it was the thirteenth day of the Hebrew month of Nisan. The Passover was to begin at sundown on that very evening. And just as Jesus gave up the ghost, and exclaimed, "*It is finished,*" the Jews all over Jerusalem were slaying their lambs for the Passover meal and placing some of their blood on the doorposts of their homes.

The blood of the first Passover was a symbol of what was to come. The blood of lambs was symbolic of the blood of the Lamb of God. When God passed over the homes of those who placed the lamb's blood on their doorposts, it represented in a symbolic way the blood of Jesus Christ which we as believers must place on the doorposts of our hearts. When God sees the blood of His Son, He does not see our sin and the destroyer passes over us.

If Egypt represented sin, then the Promised Land represented salvation. As the Israelites passed through the waters of the sea, they were in a symbolic way passing through the waters of baptism. When they passed through the water, they were dying to sin and being reborn into the promise of a better life. Again, at the end of their 40 years of wandering, the Israelites passed through the parted water of the Jordan, being baptized into the promise which God had made to Abraham.

The parting of these waters was a symbol of the baptism of Christians. When we enter the water, we die to a life of sin. When we emerge from the baptismal water, we are born again through the sacrifice of Jesus Christ and into the kingdom of God.

The Temple

The temple was a symbol of the earth. Inside were other symbolic items: the brazen laver represented the sea while the golden candlestick was symbolic of the sun. Even the clothing of the high priest was symbolic, with the breastplate set with the 12 stones representing the 12 tribes of Israel and the linen garments symbolic of purity and righteousness. His robe was decorated with pomegranates, symbol of fertility, and bells which were a warning to evil spirits. On the priest's head was a mitre which displayed the words "Holy to the Lord," which symbolized that the high priest was the extension of God's presence on earth.[1]

In the Holy of Holies rested the ark of the covenant containing the Ten Commandments, the pot of manna, and Aaron's rod. The ark of the covenant was a symbol of God's presence in that Holy Place. The lamps were fueled with pure olive oil, and the oil is the symbol of the Holy Spirit. There was also a table where the 12 loaves of showbread were placed each Sabbath. These were to represent the 12 tribes of Israel. When the old bread was removed, it could be eaten only by the priests. When Jesus instituted the Communion service, breaking the bread and giving it to the disciples, saying, "This is my body which is given for you: this do in remembrance of me," we can say the showbread was also symbolic of the body of Jesus, our Bread of Life.

Jesus used symbolism to describe our relationship with Him and with the Father. He said that He is the vine and that we are the branches. The Father is the husbandman of the vineyard.

The Cross

Christian churches display the cross as the symbol of their faith, but in actuality the cross was not used as a symbol in the Early Church. Many in the first congregations were former Jews, and to a Jew the cross represented a much too degrading symbol. For those who were steeped in Jewish culture, the statement made in Deuteronomy 21:23 which states that anyone who is hanged on a tree is cursed, was still fresh in their minds. Since the cross was to the Jews a symbol of shame and humiliation, they did not desire to have the Son of God associated with such a sign. The cross was not associated with Christianity until the fourth century A.D. and the conversion of the emperor Constantine.[2]

The Fish

The first symbol adopted by the early Christians was the

fish. Jesus had invited his disciples to become "fishers of men." The Greek word for fish was *ichthys* and the first letters in the phrase, "Jesus Christ, Son of God, Saviour" form the word *ichthys*. This symbol quickly spread through the Roman empire in the days of the Early Church, and it is likely that it became the secret symbol by which Christians identified each other during the periods of persecution by the Romans.

In biblical times there were other symbolic acts associated with secular life. When a slave was entitled to freedom but desired to stay with his master, his ear would be placed against the doorpost of the house. Then his master would drive a nail through the lobe of the slave's ear, signifying that he was now a part of the household.

Cutting one's hair when a loved one died was another fairly common practice. Since life was thought to be contained in the hair, this signified a willingness on the part of the mourner to give his own life for the loved one.

Another example of the exercise of a symbolic gesture was for a person to surrender a shoe to indicate the forfeit of all rights to personal inheritance.[3]

There has always been much symbolism in all cultures with respect to marriage. The giving of rings as indicative of lifelong devotion, the white bridal gown as a symbol of her virginity, and the throwing of rice to encourage fertility are only a few.

But to a Christian, the symbolism of the Church being the bride of Christ is most important. Unlike many human marriages of today, Jesus, the bridegroom, will never forsake His bride, and when He comes again will take her to himself forever.

7

The Parting of the Exodus Sea

When you studied American history in school, you were taught that a battle was fought on a hill overlooking Boston during the Revolutionary War. To force the British evacuation of Boston, about 1,200 American troops led by Colonel William Prescott occupied and fortified this hill on the night of June 16, 1775. At daybreak of the next day, about 3,000 British troops under the command of General William Howe attacked the hill. Colonel Prescott issued the order, "Don't shoot until you can see the whites of their eyes."

What was the name of this famous hill?

You were probably taught that it was Bunker Hill.

You were taught wrong. It was Breed's Hill.

Somehow the hills were confused after the battle and the historians chose the wrong one. But even though historians today know all about this mistake, this historic battle continues to be known by the erroneous name of Bunker Hill.

This type of error is not uncommon in history. Sometimes the attempt to write down the circumstances after the fact results in error. But in other cases, the original report is correct and the error is made in the subsequent later translation. This type of mistake, an error in translation, happened when the original Hebrew of the Book of Exodus was translated into another language over a thousand years after the event took place. This was the parting of the sea by God to allow the Israelites to escape from Pharaoh's army and safely leave Egyptian bondage.

The Exodus

The Hebrew exodus from Egypt was accompanied by a

series of extraordinary events. First there had been the plagues which had finally convinced Pharaoh to allow them to leave. In fact, he insisted on it after the "first born" of Egypt had suddenly died on the night of the first Passover.

This pharaoh, who was probably Rameses II, was at last convinced that he could no longer resist the power of the Hebrew God. His gods could not—or would not—help him. But the plagues were not the end of the demonstration of God's power.

After the Hebrews had left, Pharaoh had second thoughts about releasing them and sent his army of chariots to bring them back. He would kill Moses, who had instigated the rebellion of the slaves, and force the people to return. He badly needed the Hebrew workmen to complete the construction of his magnificent city. He also worried about his reputation among his own people. Rameses had been humiliated before his subjects. Would they still consider him a god now that he had been forced by this invisible Hebrew Lord to allow the slaves to go free? His pride would not allow that possibility.

A few days after they had left the partially-completed city of Rameses, which we now believe to be ancient Tanis, Rameses' chariots were bearing down upon the Hebrews. But God had known what Pharaoh would do and had planned to further embarrass the false gods of Egypt and the arrogant and vindictive king who ruled Egypt with a spectacular display of His awesome power.

When they had finally been allowed to leave, the Hebrews had hurriedly assembled their possessions, loading them onto carts and wagons, donkeys and whatever else they could find, to transport them out of Egypt. Then, driving their herds and flocks before them, they had followed Moses out of the land of Goshen. But where had they gone?

The Route of the Exodus

It is very important to determine exactly what route the Israelites followed when they left the city of Rameses, for this will indicate exactly where they left Egypt — and the point where the parting of the waters occurred. Scripture gives us that route. "And it came to pass, when Pharaoh had let the people go, that God led them not through the way of the land of the Philistines, although that was near; for God said, Lest peradventure the people repent when they see war, and they return to Egypt" (Exod. 13:17).

God did not lead them by way of the most direct route into Canaan, although this road near the Mediterranean Sea was close to the city of Rameses. This ancient route was heavily fortified by the Egyptians and by the Philistines in Canaan. Certainly the ferocious Philistines would not allow such a large number of people to enter their land without a battle. The Hebrews, after over 400 years of slavery, were certainly not capable of fighting as an organized army. God knew that as soon as the fighting began, these former slaves would lose their courage and run, fleeing back to the relative safety of their former bondage in Egypt. "But God led the people about, through the way of the wilderness of the Red Sea: and the children of Israel went up harnessed out of the land of Egypt" (Exod. 13:18).

This is the manner in which this verse is translated into English in our Bibles. It tells us that the Israelites were led through the way of the wilderness of the *Red Sea*. But what does the Scripture in the original Hebrew say? Let us examine the words which are translated as "Red Sea" in English to determine what these words actually mean.

> The Hebrew word for "sea" is יָם.
> The Hebrew word for "red" is אָדֹם.
> But in the Hebrew we find the sea which was parted to allow the Israelites to leave Egypt spelled יַם־סוּף
> If this were the Red Sea, then it would have been יָם־אָדֹם?
> Instead, the sea is designated by the word סוּף or *sup*.

The Hebrew words *yam sup* (pronounced yahm soof), translated here as "Red Sea," really should be translated as "Sea of Reeds."[1] If you consult Hebrew-English Old Testaments, you will find this correctly translated. The Hebrew word *sup* is derived from an Egyptian word meaning "reed." It has absolutely no connotation of any color at all, and certainly cannot mean "red."

In the Old Testament, *yam sup* is used 25 times with reference to the waters which were parted to allow the Hebrews to leave Egypt and which drowned Pharaoh's army. In every one of these Scriptures found in the Books of

Exodus, Numbers, Deuteronomy, Joshua, Judges, Nehemiah, Psalms, and Jeremiah the Hebrew text translates this as "the Sea of Reeds." Only in 1 Kings is this translated as "Red Sea" and this passage gives the location of Ezion-geber, a port which really was located on the Red Sea.

Strong's Exhaustive Concordance designates the Hebrew word *sup* as number 5,488. When we refer to this number in the Hebrew and Chaldee dictionary section of Strong's Concordance, we find the following:

5488. ‏סוף‎   çûwph, soof; prob. of Eg. or.; a reed, espec. the *papyrus*: -flag, Red (sea), weed. Comp. 5489.

5489. ‏סוף‎   çûwph, soof; for 5488 (by ellipsis of 3220); the *Reed* (Sea): - Red Sea.

The term "by ellipsis of" means that *soof* means "Red" only because it has been associated with the Red Sea. The word is correctly translated as "Reed."

What Caused This Translation Error?

The error in translation originated with the first known version of the Old Testament in a language other than Hebrew — the Septuagint, written in Greek in about 250 B.C.

This was accomplished by order of Ptolemy II Philadelphus, the second in the Ptolemaic dynasty of Egypt, who had assembled a great library at Alexandria. From the Greek-speaking Jews, Philadelphus had heard of the wisdom contained in the five books written by Moses. He desired to add these to his fabulous library of 995 volumes of the best literature from many nations.

Philadelphus sent envoys to the High Priest in Jerusalem requesting copies of these books and for men who could translate them into Greek. Even the Jews living in Alexandria had lost touch with their native language and could not help in this, nor even read much of the Torah in Hebrew.

The High Priest complied. The books and 72 scholars were sent to Egypt where they were received with high honor. Isolated on the Island of Pharos in the harbor, these men set to work translating the Hebrew books into Greek. It is possible that when the translators got to that portion of

Exodus which described the parting of the water, they inquired of the Egyptians what water it was to the southeast and by what name it was known.

But the sea which Moses and the Israelites had crossed was no longer in existence. In the centuries after the Exodus, Egyptian pharaohs had attempted to construct a canal linking the Red Sea with the Nile Delta. In the course of this construction, the Sea of Reeds had been drained, with only a few small lakes remaining. Since the only large body of water in that direction known to the Egyptians was the Red Sea, this name was used in place of the *yam sup* in the Hebrew text. In the Greek it became *Erythra Thalassa*, meaning "Red Sea."

When the Bible was translated into Latin from the Septuagint in A.D. 300 by St. Jerome, this sea became *Mare Rubrum*, again meaning "Red Sea." This Latin Vulgate Bible was subsequently used as the basis for other translations and the error continued from language to language. Biblical scholars have long been aware of this mistake in translation. Martin Luther certainly was, for he used *Schilfmeer*, meaning "Reed Sea" in his translation of the Old Testament into German.[2]

But if the Hebrews did not cross the Red Sea, where did they cross? What waters were divided to let them through to escape Pharaoh's chariots, then come crashing down to drown the Egyptian army? If we follow what the Bible tells us about their journey out of Egypt, we can determine the answers to these questions. "The children of Israel removed from Rameses, and pitched in Succoth" (Num. 33:5).

Rameses has been identified by archaeologists as the city of Tanis. Succoth is located southeast of this city. The next day their journey to freedom continued. "And they departed from Succoth, and pitched in Etham, which is in the edge of the wilderness" (Num. 33:6).

This was the second night's camp. In the morning they set off again. "And they removed from Etham, and turned again unto Pihahiroth, which is before Ballzephon: and they pitched before Migdol" (Num. 33:7-8).

This was the third night's camp. Migdol, in Hebrew, means "tower." In Egyptian texts, a fortification is referred to which archaeologists have located about 15 miles north of the modern city of Suez along the banks of a shallow marsh called the Great Bitter Lake. The Egyptian word for tower is *miktol*. Note the similarity between the name Migdol in the Bible and the Egyptian name *miktol*. The remains of this tower have been excavated.[3]

The account of their passing through the sea is continued in the next verse in the Book of Numbers. "And they departed from before Pihahiroth, and passed through the midst of the sea into the wilderness, and went three days' journey in the wilderness of Etham, and pitched in Marah" (Num. 33:8).

It was not at the Red Sea where the waters were parted, but the shallow sea which existed at that time in the area where the Great Bitter Lake now lies to the north of the Red Sea. No reeds grow along the shores of the Red Sea, but they grow in profusion in the marshes of the Bitter Lakes.

This area has changed since the time of the Exodus. The swamps and lakes are not now as extensive as they once were. The Suez Canal has partially drained this area. But these shallow lakes would have presented an impassable barrier to the Israelites as Pharaoh's chariots raced toward them. They were trapped and faced certain annihilation. This is where the hand of God parted the waters to allow His people to escape from the pursuing Egyptians, then caused the backed-up water to cascade down upon the chariots and drown the army of Pharaoh.

There is much additional evidence that this is the point where the Israelites left Egypt. We are told in Exodus 15:22-23 that after they had passed from Egypt through the parted sea, they traveled in the wilderness and found no water until they came to a place called Marah. Here they found water, but it was bitter and they could not drink it.

It has been calculated that the maximum distance they could have traveled each day, considering that many were walking and keeping the herds moving, was 15 miles. We can confirm this by measuring the distance between the camps for each of the first three days. In each case, it is approximately 15 miles.

After leaving Egypt, they traveled southward for three days to reach Marah. If they were traveling at the same pace then as they did in the first three days, they would have covered 45 miles. This is the exact distance from where the ruins of the tower have been found at *miktol* to the site that archaeologists have identified as the site of Marah.

This site is called today *Ain Hawarah* and it still contains a spring. This water is, however, not fit to drink for it is salty and has a sulfurous odor, exactly as it did when the Israelites stopped here after they had passed through the waters to leave Egypt.

From Marah, they traveled a day's journey to a place where there was good water. It was called Elim, and the scripture describes this oasis. "And they came to Elim, where were twelve wells of water, and threescore and ten palm trees: and they encamped there by the waters" (Exod. 15:27).

Fifteen miles south of *Ain Hawarah*, a day's march, is a fine oasis named *Wadi Gharandel*.[4] This oasis has many palm trees and quite a few water holes. It is very apparent that this is the biblical Elim where the Israelites did find good water after leaving the undrinkable waters of Marah.

There have been many recent archaeological discoveries giving solid evidence to substantiate events described in the Bible. Sometimes these findings throw new light on where or when the events actually took place. They can be used as a powerful witnessing tool to unbelievers who scoff at the Bible as no more than myth or legend. Modern science is Christianity's strongest ally, and we should not be fearful of revising our previously held notions of these events in the light of new discoveries. They in no way detract from the miraculous events described in the Bible, but lend scientific credibility to them.

The Waters Parted! What Happened?

After three days travel the Israelites found themselves by the shore of a body of water, extending as far in each direction as they could see. Along the banks of this sea grew papyrus reeds. This large body of water extended from a connection with the Gulf of Suez and the Red Sea northward to Lake Timsah — the Lake of Crocodiles. All that now remains of this large body of water, is Great Bitter Lake, 14 miles long and about 7 miles wide.

After allowing the Hebrews to leave, Pharaoh had a change of heart. His army of chariots was sent after them. At the shore of the Sea of Reeds they caught up with the former slaves. With the sea at their back and Pharaoh's army advancing toward them, the Israelites were trapped. But this was part of God's plan for His ultimate humiliation of the Egyptian king and his false gods. "For Pharaoh will say of the children of Israel, They are entangled in the land, the wilderness hath shut them in. And I will harden Pharaoh's heart, that he shall follow after them; and I will be honoured upon Pharaoh, and upon his host; that the Egyptians may know that I am the Lord. And they did so" (Exod. 14:3-4).

When the chariots came upon the Israelites, they found the Hebrews hemmed in against the waters of the sea. They could not escape in either direction. The Hebrews looked up in terror as the chariots bore down upon them. They shouted at Moses in anger. "... Because there were no graves in Egypt, hast thou taken us away to die in the wilderness? ..." (Exod. 14:11).

Then the angel of God, which had been leading them in a cloud, went to the rear and faced the approaching Egyptian army. There was a sudden darkness and the Egyptians could not see to continue their attack. "And Moses stretched out his hand over the sea; and the Lord caused the sea to go back by a strong east wind all that night, and made the sea dry land, and the waters were divided. And the children of Israel went into the midst of the sea upon the dry ground: and the waters were a wall unto them on their right hand, and on their left" (Exod. 14:21-22).

In the classic motion picture *The Ten Commandments,* we are shown a picture of the water instantly being parted, but this is not what Scripture tells us. God caused a strong wind to blow from the east and this wind blew all night. When the Israelites crossed over the next morning, the Lord caused the wind to stop blowing. The Egyptian chariots had started across in pursuit. "And the waters returned, and covered the chariots, and the horsemen, and all the host of Pharaoh that came into the sea after them; there remained not so much as one of them" (Exod. 14:28).

The Hebrews were now safely out of Egypt and God had dealt Pharaoh a last, humiliating blow by destroying his army. There is absolutely no doubt that it was the hand of God which accomplished this, but God used a natural force, the wind, to part the waters.

Did a miracle occur here? Yes, indeed it did! The fact that

God chose to use a natural force to part the waters makes no difference at all. God has total control over all forces of the natural world. He spoke to the wind, and the wind obeyed His command. There is another reference in the Bible where the winds obey the voice of the Creator.

Jesus fell asleep in the boat on the Sea of Galilee when a storm arose. The turbulent water terrified the disciples and the waves threatened to capsize the small ship. They awakened Jesus and He rebuked the wind. The storm immediately subsided and the wind stopped blowing. We read of the disciples amazed reaction to this. "But the men marvelled, saying, What manner of man is this, that even the wind and the sea obey him!" (Matt. 8:27).

God certainly could have parted any water He chose to part, even the extremely deep water of the Red Sea. The hundred foot walls of water that we see in *The Ten Commandments* are very dramatic but not necessary to drown Pharaoh's horsemen. A wall of water just 10 feet high would have served the purpose just as easily.

Could a wind ordered by God have caused the waters to part and allow the passage of the Israelites? In a paper published by the American Meteorological Society, Nathan Paldor and Doron Nof reported the results of their calculations which indicate that a wind blowing at 40 to 45 miles per hour for 10 hours would reduce the level of a shallow body of water by 10 feet.[5] If the wind stopped blowing abruptly, the water would then come crashing back in a few moments, causing the phenomenon which destroyed Pharaoh's army.

If the area where this occurred was joined on both sides by other large bodies of water, a wind could conceivably cause a wall of water on both sides, just as described in Exodus. This could not have happened in the Red Sea where the water is hundreds of feet deep.

Does the fact that it was the more shallow Sea of Reeds and not the deeper Red Sea diminish God's power? Certainly not! Not any more than for history to misplace the battle overlooking Boston in the American Revolution from Breeds Hill to Bunker Hill takes anything away from the courage of those brave militiamen of New England. But in order to understand the geography and history of the Exodus more perfectly, and to dispel any skeptic's questions to the possibility of its not happening, we should certainly get the location correct. The evidence indicates that it was the Sea of Reeds that was parted. But, wherever it happened, it was God's mighty hand that accomplished this miracle.

8

How Many Were in the Exodus?

When the last of the plagues had convinced Pharaoh to release the Israelites and let them leave Egypt, they quickly assembled and prepared to leave the city of Rameses. From the original 70 souls who had entered Egypt some 430 years before, they had greatly increased in number. These descendants of the sons of Jacob, along with their cattle, flocks, and herds began the journey which would 40 years later lead them into the land that God had promised to Abraham's seed.

How many Israelites left Egypt? "And the children of Israel journeyed from Rameses to Succoth, about six hundred thousand on foot that were men, beside children. And a mixed multitude went up also with them; and flocks, and herds, even very much cattle" (Exod. 12:37-38).

Six hundred thousand men — that would mean that the number of people in the families of these men would have to be added to that number. And they took with them their flocks of sheep, herds of donkeys, and their cattle. That would make a huge armada of men, women, and children and enormous numbers of animals which would have started off into the wilderness, wandering from place to place for 40 years.

Six hundred thousand men, perhaps half of them married, would mean a total of at least 900,000 men and women. If we estimate that the married couples had an average of only three children, and add this number to the 900,000, this would increase the Exodus multitude to a total of 1.8 million Israelites who went out into the desert from the city of Rameses.

If we read the biblical numbers correctly as it appears in our translations of the Bible, food and water would have had to have been provided for 1.8 million people each day for 40 years in an area in which water was at a premium and grass for grazing was sparse.

If we were to consult a military commander about what the logistics would be of moving an army of this size in desert conditions and sustaining them for only several months, we would be told that it would be an almost impossible logistical situation.

But my Bible says that this was the case!

Is my Bible wrong?

What's the answer to this seemingly impossible situation?

Could this many people have found the essential, life-sustaining water while they wandered in the desert? We shall look at just one incident after the Israelites entered the wilderness of Shur. The Book of Exodus tells us that they were without water for three days and found no water. But then they came to Marah. "And when they came to Marah, they could not drink of the waters of Marah, for they were bitter: therefore the name of it was called Marah. And the people murmured against Moses, saying, What shall we drink? And he cried unto the Lord, and the Lord shewed him a tree, which when he had cast into the waters, the waters were made sweet . . ." (Exod. 15:23-25).

The location of this water described in Exodus has been found. It is 45 miles south of the most northern tip of the Red Sea. Today this spring is called *Ain Hawarah* and the water is not very inviting, being salty and highly sulphurous. This is the bitter water described in Exodus.[1]

But God showed Moses how to make the water of this spring palatable and the multitude, thirsty after a three day's march in the wilderness and the water-skins they had brought from Rameses now empty, drank of it. They would also have had to give their cattle, sheep, and donkeys water. All of these would have had to obtain their water from one rather small spring.

How long would it have taken to satisfy the thirst of 1.8 million people from this spring of water? Let's do some calculations.

We have to make some assumptions, but we will make them overly generous. Instead of each person coming to the spring, we will estimate that one person came with a single water bag to fill, so that 20 others could share the water from that water bag. We will assume that it would take that person only one minute to fill the bag with water. And we will assume that 10 people could fill their water bags at the same time from the spring.

How long would it take to collect enough water in the water bags to satisfy the thirst of 1,800,000 people? To determine this, we multiply 1 X 20 X 10 = 200. What this means is that in each minute of time that passes, we can provide water for 200 people.

Then we divide the 1,800,000 people by 200 to see how many minutes it would take to provide water for all the people.

1,800,000 / 200 = 9,000 minutes.

There are 60 minutes in an hour, times 24 hours in a day, or 1,440 minutes in each 24 hour day.

Since it would take 9,000 minutes to provide water for all 1,800,000 people, it would take 9,000/1,440 = 6.25 days to quench the thirst of all 1,800,000 people.

If the Israelites were screaming at Moses for water after traveling just three days in the wilderness with no water, do you think some of them would be willing to wait another six days for a drink? And what about all the sheep, goats, donkeys, and cattle? They certainly had to be watered.

It would seem that the logistics would indicate that something was wrong about 1,800,000 Israelites leaving Egypt in the Exodus. And if the water supply situation was bad there, when they all had to obtain water gushing out of a rock in the desert of Zin, it would have been worse yet.

How Many Israelites Possible after 430 Years?

In the first place, all of this multitude of people are supposedly the descendants of just 70 people who came into Egypt from Canaan to escape a famine in that land. Joseph had been sold into slavery by his brothers and had achieved the second highest position in Egypt as the chief advisor to the Pharaoh. When the famine struck Canaan, his brothers came to Egypt to buy grain.

You are familiar with the Bible story. Joseph forgave them and eventually his father, Jacob, and the entire clan of 70 of his family migrated to Egypt. The 12 tribes of Israel are the descendants of the 12 sons of Jacob who came into Egypt.

Could this handful of people have produced, at the end of 430 years, descendants numbering 1,800,000 living Israelites? Is this mathematically possible? Let's do some calculations and see for ourselves.

We have to assume that half of these first 70 Israelites were men and half were women. From what we know of mortality rates of people living at that time, we find that women had a life expectancy of no more than 30 years. Childbirth in those times was extremely dangerous and many women died either during the birth of a child or from complications arising from pregnancy or delivery. "Women during those times were in a class of humanity in short supply," one observer commented. From archaeological data of burial sites, we know that parasitic diseases were major killers. Infants and children were the hardest hit and at least half of all of the population did not live past the age of 18 years.[2]

For the purpose of our calculations, we will assume that of the estimated 10 children produced from each marriage, 5 of these offspring reached the age where they could marry and reproduce. From the original 35 males and 35 females who entered Egypt, there would have been 35 X 5 = 175 living children of the first generation.

These 175 who grew to reproductive age, half male and half female, would have produced about 615 living descendants after the second generation. When we carry this progression out for the nine generations until the time of Moses, there would have been 107,438 possible descendants of the original 70 Israelites able to reproduce. But something very drastic occurred when this generation was about to reproduce. "And Pharaoh charged all his people, saying, Every son that is born ye shall cast into the river, and every daughter ye shall save alive" (Exod. 1:22).

This, of course, applied only to the Hebrews, and you know the story of Moses. When he was born, his mother hid him for three months. Then, when it was no longer possible to hide the child, she placed him in an ark of bulrushes and placed him in the Nile where Pharaoh's daughter saw him and brought the child into the palace to raise him as her own.

But few Hebrew male children were as fortunate. Some were certainly hidden and survived, but most were put to death. So in the generation of Moses, there would have been a drastic reduction in the number of male Israelites who would grow to a reproductive age.

Let us assume that 10 percent of the male children escaped from Pharaoh's death sentence. Of the 107,438, half were male. Then 107,438 X 0.5 X 0.1 = 5,372 male Hebrew children surviving to reproduce.

Moses was 80 years old at the time of the Exodus. By that time the 5,372 males would have fathered 5,372 X 5 = 26,860 offspring.

When these had grown to reproductive age, they would have produced 26,860 X .5 X 5 = 67,150 Israelites.

Now even if all of the preceding generation of 26,860 were still alive, that would mean that there was a maximum of 67,150 + 26,860 = 94,010 living Israelites at the time of the Exodus. This is a far cry from the 1,800,000 Hebrews suggested in our translation of Exodus 12:37.

Let's look at that enormous number of 1,800,000 again and see if it could possibly be realistic. From world population estimates in the *World Almanac,* we learn that the entire worldwide population at the time of the Exodus was less than 300 million people. If there really were 1.8 million Israelites in the Exodus, that means that they constituted almost 1 percent of the total population of the world.[3]

Considering the small area along the Nile that can support agriculture, it is doubtful that the Egyptian population was any more than about 2 million at the time. It is highly unlikely that the number of Israelite slaves would have almost equaled the population of native Egyptians. Only one conclusion is possible from our investigation. There could not have been 1,800,000 Israelites in the Exodus.

Is the Book of Exodus Wrong?

If the Exodus account is wrong, then how can we have confidence in other books of the Bible? If the number of Israelites in the Exodus has been grossly exaggerated, are we to believe other things that the Bible tells us? Is there any way of reconciling the number of Israelites suggested by the Exodus account with a number more realistic?

Yes! The Book of Exodus is correct. It is not the Bible which is wrong. A mistake has been made in the translation of a word.

In the Hebrew, the word which has been translated as "thousands" is *eleph*. This word is listed in *Strong's Hebrew and Chaldee Dictionary* as word number 505. According to Strong's definition, this word means "family." It could mean clan or tent group, which is an extended family. Strong's notes that this word *eventually* came to mean "thousand."[4]

But what was the meaning as it was used in Exodus 12:37? Did it mean "thousand" or did it actually mean "families" or "tent groups"? We can see the impossible situation of so many Israelites being in the Exodus if the word is correctly translated as "thousand." But if the word *eleph* in Exodus 12:37 actually stated that **600** families, or **600** tent groups comprised the Exodus, all of the impossible situations suddenly disappear.

If the word *eleph* is translated as "families," the 1,800,000 Israelites suddenly become a more logical and practical number of people. Since an extended family group could include quite a large number of individuals, the Exodus would still be a large number of Israelites. But it would be numbered in thousands and not almost two million.

This smaller traveling group would have had no problem in quenching their thirst and watering their flocks, herds, and cattle at a small spring. No longer are we faced with moving an immense army of men, women, and children through wilderness and the resultant logistical log-jam that this would entail. And we are not talking about the migration of almost 1 percent of the total population of the world at one time, a figure that is totally preposterous.

But what is more important is that we are no longer faced with doubt about the accuracy of the Book of Exodus — and with that — the entire Bible. No, the Bible is not wrong. It was a simple mis-translation of one word which has caused all of the trouble.

In other verses of Scripture, the Hebrew word *eleph* has probably been translated correctly as "thousand." But in Exodus 12: 37, I believe there should be no doubt that the correct translation is "families." God's Word is not in error, it is man who has caused the problem. I believe that what was written down by the men who wrote the books of our Bible was dictated by God, himself. Since God cannot lie, then His Word has to be true. But we are the ones who must make certain that we have the proper meaning and translation of those words.

9

What Happened to the Ark of the Covenant?

One of the Bible's greatest mysteries is what happened to the golden box which contained the original tablets of the Ten Commandments, the pot of manna, and Aaron's rod that bloomed. The Scriptures tell of the ark of the covenant being carried into Canaan, where it was before the temple was built by Solomon, and how it was placed in the Holy of Holies. But then, suddenly, all mention of this sacred object ceases.

It has been presumed by scholars that the ark was taken by Nebuchadnezzar's army when the temple was destroyed in 586 B.C. But we are not certain of that, for the ark was not listed among the sacred things that were carried off back to Babylon. What happened to this gold covered box which contained the Ten Commandments? We shall examine the evidence in this chapter and attempt to find out.

The Building of the Ark

After God had delivered His laws to Moses at Mount Sinai, He gave implicit instructions on the container they were to be kept in. "And they shall make an ark of shittim wood: two cubits and a half shall be the length thereof, and a cubit and a half the breadth thereof, and a cubit and a half the height thereof. And thou shalt overlay it with pure gold, within and without shalt thou overlay it, and shalt make upon it a crown of gold round about" (Exod. 25:10-11).

The Lord also told Moses to cast four rings, one for each corner, and to make two staffs of shittim wood to be inserted into the rings to carry the ark. God also gave instructions for something to be placed on the top of the ark. "And thou shalt make a mercy seat of pure gold: two cubits and a half shall be the length thereof, and a cubit and a half the breadth thereof. And thou shalt make two cherubims of gold, of beaten work shalt thou make them, in the two ends of the mercy seat. And make one cherub on the one end, and the other cherub on the other end: even of the mercy seat shall ye make the cherubims on the two ends thereof. And the cherubims shall stretch forth their wings on high, covering the mercy seat with their wings, and their faces shall look one to another; toward the mercy seat shall the faces of the cherubims be" (Exod. 25:17-20).

These verses raise a question: How did Moses know what a cherub looked like? There is nothing recorded about Moses asking God what cherubims were, or what their appearance might be. Apparently Moses *knew* what a cherub was and was familiar with their appearance. Unfortunately, there is much in the Bible that we would like to know, but are not specifically told.

God instructed Moses to place in the ark of the testimony all of the things that He would give Moses as commandments to the children of Israel. Two craftsmen, Bezaleel and Aholiab, were chosen by the Lord to construct the ark. Perhaps God placed in these men's minds the exact features of the cherubims and precisely how God wanted them fashioned. We are not told this, but it would be a possible explanation.

Moses had broken the original stone tablets on which God had inscribed the Ten Commandments when he had come down from Mt. Sinai and found that the Israelites had cast a golden calf and were worshipping it. God told Moses to prepare a second set of stone tablets and bring them up on the mountain. There God wrote His laws for the second time. It was these second two stone tablets containing the commandments, along with a golden pot of manna, and Aaron's rod that had budded which were placed in the ark of the covenant (Heb. 9:4). The ark was covered by a cloth of pure gold called *kaporet*.[1]

The ark was placed in the tabernacle and was moved by the Levites, who carried it by the wooden poles, whenever the Israelites moved their camp during the Exodus. The glory of the Lord was said to abide between the two cherubims, and

Aaron served the Lord before the altar in the tabernacle. When Aaron died, his son Eleazar became priest and served the Lord before the ark in the tabernacle.

At the end of the 40 years in the wilderness, when Moses had also died and Joshua had taken his place, the ark of the covenant played an important part in the Israelite entrance into the Promised Land. The Lord spoke to Joshua, giving him instructions on how the people should pass over the waters of the Jordan river and enter Canaan. "And thou shalt command the priests that bear the ark of the covenant, saying, When ye are come to the brink of the water of Jordan, ye shall stand still in Jordan" (Josh. 3:8).

Joshua gave the order. As soon as the soles of the feet of the priests who carried the ark touched the water, it stopped flowing and there was a path through the river of dry land. "Behold, the ark of the covenant of the Lord of all the earth passeth over before you into Jordan" (Josh. 3:11).

When all of the Israelites had passed through the dry river bed, the Lord told Joshua to command the priests who carried the ark to continue on to the other side. As soon as the soles of the priest's feet reached the other bank, the water of the Jordan again flowed.

The ark was used only a few days later, when it was carried by the priests around the fortress city of Jericho and the walls of this city fell. The ark was carried with the Israelites throughout the conquest of Canaan. It was first kept at Shiloh where the tabernacle was set up (Josh. 18:1). It was carried into battle until it was captured by the Philistines near Eben-Ezer (1 Sam. 4:10-11).

The ark was in the land of the Philistines for seven months. It was first taken to Ashdod and placed in the temple of their god, Dagon. There it was set up, but the next morning when the priests of Dagon entered the temple they found the statue of Dagon had fallen. They were astonished to see that Dagon's statue was now face down on the floor in front of the ark of the God of Israel.

They set up the idol again, but the next morning found it fallen again before the ark. But this time, the head and both hands of the statue had broken off (1 Sam. 5:1-4). The city of Ashdod was stricken with a plague and the inhabitants were terrified. They insisted that the ark of the God of Israel be removed from their city, convinced that its presence had caused the plague.

The ark was carried to Gath, which also suffered from a plague as soon as the ark had arrived. The citizens of Gath demanded that it be removed. It was next taken to Ekron, but when the inhabitants saw the ark approaching their city, they were furious."Therefore they sent the ark of God to Ekron. And it came to pass, as the ark of God came to Ekron, that the Ekronites cried out, saying, They have brought about the ark of the God of Israel to us, to slay us and our people" (1 Sam. 5:10).

All the chief men of the Philistines gathered together to decide what to do with the ark. They could do only one thing, return the ark to the Israelites or continue to suffer the consequences. It was returned, but not without incident (1 Sam. 6:1-21). The ark was finally back in Israel and was kept in the house of Abinadab in Kirjath-jearim, where his son, Eleazar, was sanctified to keep it. The ark rested here for about 20 years.

David finally brought the ark to Jerusalem where it was stored in a tent. When Solomon built the temple, it was installed there with great ceremony (1 Kings 8:1-10). This was in about the year 870 B.C. There is no mention of the ark until about the year 640 B.C. when Josiah repaired the temple which had been neglected under the evil kings of Judah (2 Chron. 35:3).

In 586 B.C. Nebuchadnezzar's army captured Jerusalem, destroyed the temple, and carried the sacred objects contained in it back to Babylon (2 Kings 25:13-17). There was, however, no mention made specifically of the ark of the covenant among the things that were carried off to Babylon. Nor is there any mention of the ark in the list of sacred items returned to Jerusalem after the captivity was over. The second temple does not appear to have contained the ark.

Was the ark still in Solomon's Temple at the time of the Babylonian conquest and the destruction of Solomon's Temple? Or had it been removed sometime before? There are conflicting stories about what happened to the ark. We will examine these conflicting accounts and try to determine where the ark, if it still exists, might be at this present time.

What Happened to the Ark?

It may be that it was indeed still in the temple at the time of the Babylonian conquest of Jerusalem. It may have been carried back and the gold removed from it and melted down. Other items, however, which also were made of precious metals, remained intact and were restored to the Jews when Cyrus allowed them to return and construct another House of the Lord.

The ark of the covenant was such a unique thing that it is difficult to imagine that Nebuchadnezzar would destroy it just to melt down the gold overlay and the beaten gold of the cherubims. He did not do this with much more ordinary items such as pots, shovels, and other temple objects which were also fashioned from precious metals.

One of the books of the Apocrypha, 2 Maccabees, tells us that Jeremiah took the ark from Jerusalem and hid it in a cave on Mt. Nebo, where Moses had been buried. This book, however, claims to be a condensation in a single book of a five volume history written by Jason of Cyrene in about 110 B.C. The records referred to in 2 Maccabees concerning what Jeremiah did with the ark are unknown.

What this book of the apocrypha states is:

> It was also in the writing that the prophet, having received an oracle, ordered that the tent and the ark should follow with him, and that he went out to the mountain where Moses had gone up and had seen the inheritance of God. And Jeremiah came and found a cave, and he brought there the tent and the ark and the altar of incense, and he sealed up the entrance. Some of those who followed him came up to mark the way, but could not find it. When Jeremiah learned of it he rebuked them and declared: 'The place shall be unknown until God gathers his people together again and shows his mercy. And then the Lord will disclose these things, and the glory of the Lord and the cloud will appear, as they were shown in the case of Moses, and as Solomon asked that the place should be specially consecrated' (2 Maccabees 2:1-8).

There is a verse in Jeremiah which some have used to support this theory of what happened to the ark. However, this verse may be used also to mean that Jeremiah either knew that the ark was missing from the temple, or that he expected Nebuchadnezzar's army, which would soon lay siege to the city, to remove it. "And it shall come to pass, when ye be multiplied and increased in the land, in those days, saith the Lord, they shall say no more, The ark of the covenant of the Lord: neither shall they remember it; neither shall they visit it; neither shall that be done any more" (Jer. 3:16).

Did Jeremiah remove the ark of the covenant from the temple? That is difficult to believe knowing the conditions at the time.

Jeremiah was not in favor with the priests, and without their cooperation, it could not have been taken from the temple.

Jeremiah was preaching that the Babylonians were the force which God had raised up to punish Judah and that the city should not resist them. The priests, on the other hand, were predicting a victory over the armies of Babylon. They said that God would certainly not allow His city, and especially His temple, to be overthrown by the pagans from beyond the rivers.

It would have been almost impossible for Jeremiah to gain access to the Holy of Holies, remove the ark, and transport it unnoticed by the priests outside the walls of the city and take it across the Jordan to Mt. Nebo. It is an interesting story, and many men have explored the mountain of Moses in an attempt to locate the cave containing the ark of the covenant. Of course, no such cave has been located.

Another explanation of what happened to the ark, and one with a more plausible scenario, states that the priests hid the ark in the tunnel system which exists on Mt. Moriah. We do know that there are extensive tunnels carved from the rock underneath the place where the temple once stood.

When the crusaders conquered Jerusalem, they discovered these subterranean passageways and explored them. They were also familiar with the legends concerning the hiding of the ark by the priests before the Babylonians breached the walls of Jerusalem. They found no trace of the ark of the covenant.

Recently there have been claims made that two Israelis gained entry to the tunnel system beneath the Temple Mount and had seen the ark. The men say that when they returned, the Moslems had sealed off the entrance they had used to the passageway.

This was exciting news to many, but it strains the comprehension how two men could quickly locate the ark in the same tunnels in which the crusaders had searched unsuccessfully during almost a hundred years of occupation.

A very colorful Ethiopian legend concerning what happened to the ark is found in the *Kebra Nagast*, an Ethiopian literary work which was written somewhere between the sixth and ninth centuries A.D. This writing claims that the ark of the covenant, *tabot* in classical Ethiopic, was brought to Ethiopia by Menelik, the alleged son of Solomon and the Queen of Sheba. At the same time, according to the legend, the Jewish religion was introduced into the country. It is true that the word *tabot* is derived from the Jewish-Aramaic word *tebuta* and is related to the Hebrew word *tebah*, meaning "ark" or "box."[2]

In fact, Ethiopian Christians and Jews both claim that the ark of the covenant still rests in that country, in the Church of Mary Zion in the city of Aksum. While the tale told in the *Kebra Nagast* concerning Menelik bringing the ark back from Jerusalem may be far-fetched, there is another recently developed scenario which has considerable merit.

A young journalist, Graham Hancock, has traced what he believes to be the path of the ark of the covenant when it left the temple in Jerusalem. In his book he claims that sometime between when the Bible last mentions the ark during the reign of Josiah and the Babylonian conquest, the priests in charge of the ark removed it. This, Hancock states, was because the kings of Judah were evil and these priests either foresaw God's wrath descending upon Jerusalem or they considered the ark too sacred to remain in such an evil nation.

Hancock traces the ark first to the island of Elephantine, 500 miles to the south, in Egypt. There are ruins on this island which are definitely a temple, and the only Jewish temple known outside of Jerusalem. It is well known that Jews did inhabit Elephantine at that time and had a well-established community. Hancock believes that the ark was hidden here.

There seems to be ruins of a sacrificial altar on Elephantine Island and he believes that this played a part in the
eventual removal of the ark from Egypt. Since the Jews
sacrificed rams, and one of the Egyptian gods was Anukis,
who was pictured with the head of a ram, there was animos-
ity between the Jews and Egyptians. Hancock believes this
led to the removal of the ark from Egypt, perhaps in haste for
fear of an Egyptian attack on the temple.

He traces the passage of the ark down the Nile by ship to
Dembi Dolo in Ethiopia. More Jewish ruins are to be found
here, also with what appears to be sacrificial altars. Local oral
tradition in the area claims that the ark was indeed kept at
Dembi Dolo, and remained there for 800 years until Ethiopia
was converted to Christianity in about A.D. 350.

At that time the ark was moved to the city of Aksum
where it was installed in the church of Mary Zion. In his book,
Hancock states that only one holy man is allowed to enter the
chapel where the ark is kept and no one is permitted to as
much as see it. Each Christian church in Ethiopia does,
however, contain a replica of the ark and this is carried
through the streets during festival parades. The Ethiopian
church has always claimed that the original ark of the covenant actually does rest in the church of Mary Zion.

Graham Hancock may or not be correct, and we cannot
know for certain until whatever is inside the chapel at the
church in Aksum is examined. But his work in tracing the
missing ark of the covenant fills in a substantial number of the
pieces of the puzzle which has surrounded the disappear-
ance of the ark.[3]

One cannot help wondering whether God will reveal
this sacred treasure to a skeptical and Bible-scoffing world.
Wouldn't it be a tremendous testimony to the truth of God's
Word, the Holy Bible, for both arks to be found: Noah's ark
on Mt. Ararat and the ark of the covenant — wherever it
might be?

10

What Did God Have against Pigs? God's Dietary Laws Made Sense

Not long after the Israelites were brought out of Egyptian bondage, the Lord gave Moses the primary laws under which the people should live. These Ten Commandments were engraved by God on stone tablets. But these laws did not cover the everyday life of people in areas such as worship, personal hygiene, and what they could or could not eat and drink. After the portable tabernacle had been constructed, God added these rules and ordinances, giving them orally to Moses.

The book which we know as Leviticus contains the written record of what God expected of His people, how they were to worship Him, what sacrifices to offer for special occasions, and how to live the holy and righteous life He expected of them.

God had definite rules on what the Hebrews could eat and what was to be strictly prohibited. These dietary laws were recorded in the eleventh chapter of Leviticus. Only certain animals, fish, fowl, and insects were considered "clean" and could be eaten. There was no prohibition on any kind of fruit or vegetables.

But not all parts of the "clean" animals could be eaten. The Hebrews were not to consume blood from any acceptable meat, and certain organs of these animals were not to be eaten. These dietary laws were later to include the separation of types of food so that dairy products and meat were neither eaten at the same time nor prepared in the same vessels. This was called *kosher*, from the Hebrew word meaning "fitting" or "proper," and included the slaughter of the animal by humane methods; the draining of the blood; and washing, salting, and soaking meat to remove all possible traces of blood.

In order not to violate these laws, Jews did not eat in the houses of Gentiles, for fear that the dishes would be contaminated by preparing or serving both dairy products and meat in the same pots. They were also concerned about eating meat that had been in some way blessed by the pagan gods of the unbelievers. It was the dietary restriction more than anything else that kept Jews and Gentiles from associating with one another.

These dietary laws were not required of Christians, even Jews who were the first followers of Jesus. After Peter was given a vision of all of the "unclean" foods and told by God to eat them, he had protested, ". . . Not so, Lord; for I have never eaten anything that is common or unclean. And the voice spake unto him again the second time, What God hath cleansed, that call not thou common" (Acts 10:14-15).

But many Christians of today, when asked what they know about the Jewish dietary laws, would immediately reply, "Jews can't eat pork." Many of us know this, even if we know nothing of the rest of the *kosher* laws. That leads us to the question, "What did God have against pigs? Why did He forbid the Hebrews to eat pork?"

Why God Wanted No Pigs

I had always been told that the reason the Lord forbade the eating of pork was because of the possibility of the Hebrews contracting the parasite which causes trichinosis if the meat is not thoroughly cooked. It is true that many pigs do carry the larvae of *Trichinella spiralis* and that insufficiently cooked pork can pass this larvae to man, where it reaches maturity in the intestines. The mature worm then gives birth to multitudes of larvae which are carried in the lymph and blood to the muscles where they become encysted. This causes severe pain, swelling, fever, and even prostration.

But trichinosis was not primarily why God did not want

the Israelites around pigs. There is a much more serious and potentially deadly reason. Pigs are perfect incubators for epidemics caused by viruses. Within the pig, mutations can take place in these viruses, making them deadly to man.

It has been discovered that many epidemics are carried around the world by migratory birds, especially waterfowl. These organisms are not harmful to the birds who carry them in their intestines. And they would not usually be pathogenic to man — unless a mutation occurs — or the genes of the virus happens to get crossed with a virus from a human.

A good example of this is Asian flu. Each year as the birds migrate, they carry the influenza virus from Asia to other parts of the globe. Birds being birds, they litter the ground along the migratory route with their droppings. Humans rarely come in contact with bird excrement — but pigs do. As a pig eats its food from the ground, it also ingests the bird droppings.

Pigs are exposed to viruses from their keepers. Any virus a man or a bird can catch, a pig can catch, too. Usually, bird viruses do not replicate well in humans and human viruses do not replicate well in birds. But both do very well in pigs.

When both a human virus and a bird virus infect the same cell of a pig's respiratory tract and both begin to rearrange the cell's genetic material to duplicate their own, the genes can get crossed between them. A team of Italian and American virologists have been investigating this for 12 years and show that this can happen. What results is a new and sometimes much more virulent strain than either virus had previously been.

Humans transmit a virus infection by coughing, distributing airborne viruses to those nearby. Astonishingly, pigs also cough. When the bird-human virus is coughed or breathed into the air by the pig, humans are infected with the mutant strain. They then spread the new virus to humans.[1]

According to virologist Robert Webster, who led the American half of the research team, these findings prove that pigs do indeed act as the mixing vessels for the transfer of avian-carried viruses to man. "Pigs are perfect mixing vessels," says Dr. Webster, "and may well be the source of the next pandemic.

"All subtypes of influenza occur naturally in waterfowl," says Dr. Webster. "They are the ultimate reservoir of influenza. These strains usually can't infect people, but some may infect pigs, as can some human flu strains. So if a pig becomes infected with two virus strains — one from water-fowl, one from humans — simultaneously, their genetic information can mix to give a duck-human strain. We can postulate that the human epidemic began when a farmer caught the new virus while tending his pigs."[2]

I believe this is the reason that God did not allow the Israelites to keep pigs. It would have taken only one large-scale epidemic to wipe out the relatively small group of Hebrews. It was not that the Lord didn't like pork chops, but strictly for health reasons that He forbade the Israelites to keep pigs.

Other Forbidden Animals

Any animal that had a parted hoof and chewed its cud could be eaten. This meant that the Hebrews could eat the animals which they had been keeping either to work, such as oxen, or the cattle, sheep, and goats from their herds. They could also hunt deer and other related game species.

But God specifically prohibited them from eating certain other beasts such as the camel, the hare, and the coney — the rock hyrax that looks like a rabbit-sized guinea pig, weasels, ferrets, mice, chameleons, lizards, snails, and moles. The donkey, used as a beast of burden, would also be excluded.

Most of these forbidden animals were scavengers. The camel had not yet been domesticated or tamed at this time. It was not until about 1100 B.C. that the camel was used as a beast of burden, which allowed men to cross the arid and desolate regions of desert carrying on commerce between distant civilizations. Perhaps God was concerned the wild camels carried disease. Certainly those animals which ate carrion would be a threat, and there is good reason not to eat them.

Mice can carry deadly pathogens. The recent mysterious illness which killed a dozen people in the southwestern United States has been traced to the Hantaan virus, a usually fatal hemorrhagic fever, carried by field mice. This virus is diagnosed in over 100,000 cases each year in China alone. It is not a new disease. It has been described in ancient Chinese medical texts which are over a thousand years old.³ Certainly this disease existed in biblical times. Mice carry other pathogenic organisms such as Junin, which causes a painful and sometimes fatal type of hemorrhagic fever.

Weasels, ferrets, chameleons, lizards, and snails feed on other animals or carrion, and would also be a health threat. The dead body of animals decays quickly, allowing a proliferation of growth of all kinds of bacteria. Any scavenger which feeds on dead carcasses also ingests these bacteria, some of which may have killed the dead animal itself.

It is interesting to note that all of the animals God allowed the Hebrews to eat were those which ate grass or grain. This diet minimized the possibility of the animal picking up infectious agents from what it consumed.

Also forbidden were any animals that go about on their bellies such as snakes and worms.

Fish and Seafood

"Whatsoever hath no fins nor scales in the waters, that shall be an abomination unto you" (Lev. 11:12). The Hebrews were restricted to fish that had scales and fins. This eliminated such fish as eels, frogs and all shellfish, lobsters, crabs, and shrimp. Eels and crabs are scavengers, so their inclusion in the list of forbidden seafood is for much the same reason as animal scavengers.

Shellfish such as oysters and clams are known to carry pathogens which can cause such ailments as hepatitis, especially when eaten raw. They also spoil very quickly without adequate refrigeration. The Hebrews had no means of refrigeration. In fact, the only means of storing food such as fish was by salting and drying them. Fish are easily preserved in this manner and this method is used even today with some species.

God's dietary restrictions on seafood made good medical sense for the Israelites. They were for the purpose of keeping these people healthy and away from potential sources of pathogenic bacteria. Only God, who created all living things, would have known which foods were safe and which could be dangerous.

Fowls, Birds, and Flying Things

Today when we consider flying things which are edible,

we naturally think only of birds. But there are other creatures which fly, and these are included in the diets of many people in the world. In some cultures grasshoppers are a delicacy. In biblical times, people often ate things which we would not consider for our own tables. God had to take all of this into consideration when the laws concerning flying things were given to the Hebrews.

First God dealt with birds and fowl. Specifically prohibited were the eagle, the ossifrage, the osprey, the raven, vultures, the kite, owls, nighthawks, the cuckoo, the cormorant, pelicans, swans, the heron, the lapwing, and the bat. These are primarily birds of prey. Many feed on creatures such as mice from which they could become carriers of the same diseases for which mice were forbidden. Others are scavengers, feasting on the rotting carrion of carcasses. To eat scavengers would certainly be an extreme health hazzard.

Clean birds would include pigeons, doves, and sparrows. Quail must have also been considered clean, for God provided them to the Israelites in abundance at one instance during the Exodus. No mention is made of eggs being clean or unclean, but instructions are given in Deuteronomy 22:6 not to kill a mother bird when eggs are taken from her nest.

Flying things other than birds are also addressed. In many parts of the world today, insects are a part of a normal diet and apparently this was true in biblical times. Leviticus refers to insects as flying creeping things. Insects which the Hebrews were permitted to eat were restricted to beetles and grasshoppers. Locusts are grasshoppers, of the family *Acridiidae,* which have become migratory.

When grasshoppers reproduce too rapidly for the food supply, they undergo extensive changes in external form and become migratory. Actually, locusts are grasshoppers who are facing starvation and have been forced to find another area where food is more plentiful. They become eating machines, swarming into areas where food may be found and consuming everything edible. As long as there have been grasshoppers on earth, there have been plagues of locusts denuding the land.

Other Laws

Not only were many animals, birds, water creatures, and

insects considered unclean as far as food, their dead carcasses were not to be touched or the person coming in contact with them would be unclean and require purification. Cooking pots and utensils made of wood, skin, or similar materials which came in contact with the carcasses of unclean creatures had to be thoroughly washed before use. If an earthen vessel was contaminated, it was to be broken and never used again.

If any animal which was permitted for food died of natural causes, it was considered unclean and could not be touched. If a person came into contact with it, that person had to wash himself and would not be considered clean until that evening.

A strange statement is made in three places concerning how food should be prepared. In Exodus 23:19; again in 34:26; and also in Deuteronomy 14:21 we find the commandment: "Thou shalt not seethe a kid in his mother's milk." It was from these words that would also come the prohibition against mixing any foods containing meat with dairy products. This is a significant element of what it means for a Jew to "keep kosher."

Although Scripture calls only for not boiling a kid in the milk of its mother, Jewish rabbis were later to construct what is called "a fence around the law" and interpret this single, rather narrow prohibition as forbidding *any* dairy product at all to be eaten with *any* meat dish. This was also later expanded to prohibit any pot, bowl, or utensil which was used to prepare meat from being used at any time to contain any dairy product. As a result, kosher Jews must maintain two separate sets of all cooking equipment, one for meat and another for dairy foods.

But the basis for the commandment itself has been a puzzle to biblical scholars. Why would the Israelites even have contemplated boiling a young goat in the milk from the goat from which it had been born? In *The Guide to the Perplexed*, Maimonides suggested a possible answer to this question.

"As for the prohibition against eating meat (boiled) in milk, it is my opinion not improbable that — in addition to this being undoubtedly very gross food and very filling — idolatry had something to do with it. Perhaps such food was eaten at one of the ceremonies of their cult or one of their festivals. Although this is the most probable view regarding the reason for this prohibition, I have not seen this set down in any of the books of the Sabeans (pagans) that I have read."

Mainmonides deduced that the reason this practice was forbidden was because the Canaanites may have done this in their pagan ceremonies and festivals. Some substantiation was given to this view when the royal library of tablets was discovered at Ugarit by French archaeologist Claude Schaeffer. One of these tablets was translated to reveal a statement which seemed to say, *"Cook a kid in milk."* Biblical commentators quickly made use of this and it has been generally accepted that the reason for this prohibition was that it was part of pagan worship. The Canaanite practice was thought to have been widespread and perhaps part of some fertility rite. Naturally, the Israelites would be commanded not to follow such pagan practices, hence the warning in the Pentateuch.

Jacob Milgrom, professor of Hebrew and Bible at the University of California at Berkeley, writing in *Bible Review,* has brought to light a different reason. He states that the tablet found at Ugarit has been erroneously translated and has nothing to do with either "cooking" or "milk" and probably not even a "kid." Dr. Milgrom believes the prohibition against seething a kid in his mother's milk is in accord with other laws showing a reverence for life and a separation of life and death. Milk, the life-sustaining nourishment of the young animal, should never be associated with that young animal's death.[4]

No matter what the reason for this prohibition, it has become the basis for a major part of the Jewish dietary laws. The rabbis, by building what is called a "fence around the law," insured that no Jew would ever boil a kid in its mother's milk by strictly prohibiting any meat and milk from being either prepared or eaten together. Apparently it has worked very well.

Food Preservation

The Israelites certainly had no ice for refrigeration. They could not "can" food. The only manner of keeping food fit for later consumption was drying and salting it. Salt preserves food, but even now the scientific understanding of how salt inhibits food spoilage is not completely understood.

It is known that high levels of salt are toxic to most cells, including bacteria. If food is preserved using salt, any bacteria settling on it will absorb salt. The bacteria cell will then have to expend considerable energy in pumping the salt back out of itself. In many bacteria, this drains so much energy from the bacteria that it must shut down other functions, such as producing toxins, or in cell division, which would produce more bacteria.

Robert L. Buchanan of the U.S. Agriculture Department's Eastern Research Center in Philadelphia has found that sodium chloride also reduces the bacteria's ability to absorb food, placing further strain on its energy system. It is also possible that the salt also alters the ability of negatively charged bacteria to adhere to the positively charged surfaces of salted meat.[5]

Salt was a valuable commodity to ancient people. Many trade routes were established to carry cakes of salt to areas where it could not be otherwise obtained. The Israelites were fortunate, for salt was plentiful along the shores of the Salt Sea or by evaporating water from the Mediterranean.

Today we tend to severely restrict the amount of salt in our diets, but the Israelites were a hard-working people in a very hot climate. They must have lost quite a lot of salt each day through perspiration, and needed an almost daily quantity of salt in the diet to maintain their electrolytes. Salt is mentioned about 35 times in the Bible, so perhaps God knew that they needed it. In any event, it did not seem to harm them.

Personal Hygiene

The Israelites were a clean people. They washed their food thoroughly before it was prepared. They washed their hands both before and after eating. Bathing was a ritual. With any sign of disease, they were commanded to wash their clothing with water as well as their bodies. Other laws such as circumcision and dealing with communicable diseases such as leprosy by segregation of those who had it, prevented the spread of certain types of illness.

God's Laws Made Good Sense

When we first look at the dietary laws under which the

Israelites were forced to live, they seem to be very restrictive. But on closer examination, these laws made extremely good sense. Today we are advised that a low-fat, low-cholesterol diet is good for us. We are told to exercise and to get plenty of rest. That's exactly what God's laws prescribed for the Hebrews.

Meat was not a daily item on their menu. In fact, it was probably only on special feast days that the Israelites ate any meat at all. What their diet did include was plenty of fruit and vegetables. Protein came from legumes. Certainly their daily work provided them all with more than adequate exercise. Wherever they went, they had to walk. The Sabbath was reserved for worship and rest.

Bread was indeed their very staff of life, eaten at every meal and used as the eating utensil itself. Most foods were boiled together in a single pot over the fire. Other fruits were eaten raw. It was a diet high in complex carbohydrates and low in saturated fats. Animal organs such as the liver and kidneys were forbidden and the fat of animals was reserved for sacrifice. Blood was strictly prohibited.

Seafood which would quickly spoil, such as shellfish, were not allowed. Pigs, which have been shown to be a major source of epidemic disease, were not only forbidden to be eaten but no Israelite could as much as go near them. Olive oil was used for cooking and honey was the only available sweetener. Among the Israelites, as with other cultures of the time, mothers nursed their children for several years.

The dietary laws set forth in Leviticus make extraordinary good *scientific* sense. Since these were given by God, we would certainly expect them to. God wanted the very best for the people He had chosen, not only to worship Him, but to eventually bring forth His Son into this world. His dietary laws, as do all of His other laws governing how we should live, make perfect sense.

These laws kept the Israelites away from pigs, the carriers of the infectious diseases which could have wiped them out in one violent episode. They ate little red meat and no fat, a very healthy low-cholesterol diet. The grain which produced their bread contained the bran fiber. Recent studies have shown that two ounces of wheat bran each day caused premalignant colon polyps to shrink.

The dietary laws dictated that the Hebrews ate plenty of vegetables and fruit, both containing high amounts of anti-oxidants such as beta-carotene, folate, and lutein. They ate much garlic, leeks, and onions. A recent German study indicates that a particular garlic compound, ajoene, actually is toxic to malignant cells and may also boost the body's immune functions. Sulfur compounds found in garlic have been found to increase the activity of macrophages and T-lymphocytes which destroy cancer cells.

Oranges, lemons, grapefruit, and limes all contain natural substances such as carotenoids and flavonids that have been found to neutralize chemical carcinogens.

Who else but the Creator of mankind would be able to prescribe the ideal diet for His creation's best health? In a time when such scientific facts were completely unknown, only God could have made these dietary laws which would give good health, long life, and vitality to His people. The dietary laws did indeed make sense!

11

Why Did God Bury Moses Himself?

After the Israelites had languished in Egyptian slavery for over 400 years, God selected a man to lead them out of their captivity and prepare them to enter the land that He had promised to them as descendants of Abraham. This man, Moses, was to have a very special relationship with God throughout the next 40 years. This was evident from the very first, for God told Moses that he would be as a god in Pharaoh's eyes. "And the Lord said unto Moses, See, I have made thee a god to Pharaoh: and Aaron thy brother shall be thy prophet" (Exod. 7:1).

Through Moses, God sent a series of 10 plagues upon Egypt. But after each of the first nine, God hardened Pharaoh's heart and he refused to allow the Israelites to leave. The last plague, which killed the "first born" of the land was too much even for Pharaoh. He relented and gave Moses permission to take his people out of Egypt.

But even then, God hardened Pharaoh's heart again and the king sent his chariots out to bring back his former slaves and to kill Moses. When the Egyptian troops had found the Israelites camped next to the sea, and with all avenues of escape cut off, God performed another miracle and parted the water. After the Israelites had successfully crossed over on dry land, the waters swallowed the pursuing Egyptian chariots.

Again and again God gave evidence of His power by producing water from rocks, sweetening bitter water for them to drink, and providing food in a barren land. Each time it was through Moses that God performed these miracles. Moses became the ultimate judge of disputes among the people and his word was to be instantly obeyed.

When a revolt broke out against Moses, God caused the ground to open up and swallow Korah and those who had joined him in the rebellion against Moses.

It was Moses who ascended Mt. Sinai to receive the Ten Commandments written by the finger of God on the tablets. It was Moses to whom God gave the instructions concerning the building of the tabernacle. Moses heard the voice of God and received the ordinances and laws by which God expected the Israelites to live.

No human being since Adam had enjoyed the intimacy with God in the manner that Moses was privileged to do. And in his people's eyes, Moses was being elevated far beyond the realm of a mortal human being.

It was in the desert of Zin that Moses' sister Miriam died and was buried. But in this place there was no water and the people murmured again against Moses and Aaron. Moses and Aaron left the assembly of complainers and fell on their faces before the door of the tabernacle. Then the Lord spoke to Moses: "Take the rod, and gather thou the assembly together, thou, and Aaron thy brother, and speak ye unto the rock before their eyes; and it shall give forth his water, and thou shalt bring forth to them water out of the rock: so thou shalt give the congregation and their beasts drink" (Num. 20:8).

Moses took the rod and gathered the people before the rock. "And Moses and Aaron gathered the congregation together before the rock, and he said unto them, Hear now, ye rebels; must we fetch you water out of this rock? And Moses lifted up his hand, and with his rod he smote the rock twice: and the water came out abundantly, and the congregation drank, and their beasts also" (Num. 20:10-11).

But the Lord was not pleased and He spoke to Moses and Aaron. ". . . Because ye believed me not, to sanctify me in the eyes of the children of Israel, therefore ye shall not bring this congregation into the land which I have given them" (Num. 20:12).

Why was God displeased with Moses and Aaron? What did they do that caused God to take away from them the honor of leading the people into the Promised Land? I had always heard that it was because Moses struck the rod instead of speaking to it. But I think that there was something more involved than this.

Notice in this verse of Scripture that Moses uses the plural "we." Who was Moses referring to beside himself? It could certainly have been Aaron, but I don't think it was. I believe that Moses was referring to God. What Moses was actually doing was placing himself along side of God as an equal. That, I am convinced, was why the Lord was displeased with Moses. Moses had taken equal credit with God for providing the water to the Israelites.

God told Moses that he had not sanctified the Lord in the eyes of the children of Israel. There is no way that God will share His glory with any mortal man, not even the greatest of the prophets. "I am the Lord: that is my name: and my glory will I not give to another, neither my praise to graven images" (Isa. 42:8).

The punishment that Moses received was not to lead the people into the Promised Land. God would not allow him to enter it himself. At the end of the 40 years of wandering, the Israelites approached the Jordan River across from Jericho. That day the Lord spoke again to Moses. "Get thee up into this mountain Abarim, unto mount Nebo, which is in the land of Moab, that is over against Jericho; and behold the land of Canaan, which I give unto the children of Israel for a possession: And die in the mount whither thou goest up, and be gathered unto thy people; as Aaron thy brother died in mount Hor, and was gathered unto his people: Because ye trespassed against me among the children of Israel at the waters of Meribah-Kadesh, in the wilderness of Zin; because ye sanctified me not in the midst of the children of Israel" (Deut. 32:49-51).

And Moses went up into the mountain and the Lord showed him all the land which had been given to the former slaves which had been led out of Egyptian captivity, land that been promised to the seed of Abraham. And Moses died there on Mount Nebo. And God himself buried Moses. "And he buried him in a valley in the land of Moab, over against Bethpeor: but no man knoweth of his sepulcher unto this day" (Deut. 34:6).

Why did the Lord bury Moses, himself? Why didn't God allow Moses to die among his own people and be buried by them? Why did the Lord hide the burial place of this great prophet?

It is said that Moses was the most humble man that ever lived. But what man, no matter how humble he might be, could fail to feel some measure of greatness in the stature to which God had elevated him? Without a doubt, Moses was the greatest of all the prophets to arise out of Israel. "And there arose not a prophet since in Israel like unto Moses, whom the Lord knew face to face" (Deut. 34:10).

If Moses had been buried by the people that he had led out of Egypt, what do you think would have happened to his grave? This man had been a "savior" to his people. He had led them out of slavery into their own land, a land in which they would prosper. He had cared for them as a father cares for his children. And the people deeply loved and revered Moses. When he died, the children of Israel wept for Moses for 30 days.

If the burial place of Moses were known today, don't you believe that there would be a shrine built at its location? Jews today honor and revere him as their law giver. The law which God gave to them through Moses is not called the Law of God. Instead it is called the Law of Moses.

If his burial place had been known, there may even have been a temple built upon it — dedicated not to God — but to the man, Moses. Lesser men than Moses have inspired such hero worship, and some have been almost deified by followers. Moses would certainly not have wanted such a thing to occur, but it could well have happened.

Satan would have liked for Moses burial place to have been known. In fact, the devil fought to have the location known so that this man's sepulcher would have been made a shrine where his memory could have been worshipped by misguided Jews. Satan would have liked nothing better than to draw attention away from God toward a mortal man.

We are told in the Book of Jude that Satan bitterly contested the body of Moses. "Yet Michael the archangel, when contending with the devil he disputed about the body of Moses, durst not bring against him a railing accusation, but said, The Lord rebuke thee" (Jude 9).

But God had not forgotten the great service of the man who was faithful for so many years. The fact that Moses has a high place in heaven is attested to in Scripture. At the Mount of Transfiguration, when Jesus took Peter, John, and James with Him and was transfigured before them, the disciples saw two other figures talking with Jesus. "And, behold, there talked with him two men, which were Moses and Elias" (Luke 9:30).

Peter wanted to build three tabernacles on the mountain in honor of Moses, Elias, and Jesus. But again God indicates that mortal men are not to share divine glory. A cloud overshadowed them and a voice came from heaven, saying, "This is my beloved son: hear him." It was Jesus who was to be glorified: not Moses, not Elias — no one but God.

Unfortunately, there are contemporary parallels to the elevation of men to a godlike status. Remember the tragedy of the followers of James Jones, who were convinced that he was God, and committed mass suicide on his order. More recently the events at Waco, Texas, where the Branch Davidians belief of David Koresh's claim to be Jesus Christ led to a flaming death for many men, women, and children. These are just two such parallels. Sadly, there are Christian ministries today where the leader is held in a similar exalted and almost deified state.

God is not willing to share His glory with any mortal man. If Moses, who in a second of time and with one slip of his tongue, was punished by the Lord for not giving Him the total glory, consider the fate of those who delight in basking in the admiration of their overzealous followers. God is not about to share His glory with any mortal man.

12

The Mysterious Urim and Thummim

Although God spoke directly to Moses, and perhaps also to some of the later prophets, there was another way in which God communicated with and directed the actions of the Israelites. This was by use of the mysterious objects known as the Urim and Thummim.

The Scripture tells us very little about the Urim and Thummim. We must glean from only seven verses of the Bible what little we can say with any degree of confidence about these objects and how they were used.

We know that God ordained their use. When Moses was given instructions concerning the breastplate that Aaron, the high priest, was to wear when he stood before the Lord in the Tabernacle, the Urim and Thummim were to be placed in the breastplate. "And thou shalt put in the breastplate of judgment the Urim and the Thummim; and they shall be upon Aaron's heart, when he goeth in before the Lord: and Aaron shall bear the judgment of the children of Israel upon his heart before the Lord continually" (Exod. 28:30).

When Aaron went in before the Lord, he wore the holy garments which God had specified. These included the ephod, the robe, an embroidered coat, a mitre, and a girdle. In addition, Aaron wore an elaborate breastplate on which were 12 stones, each representing one of the 12 tribes of Israel. God told Moses to place the Urim and the Thummim in the breastplate, next to Aaron's heart when he went in before the Lord.

It is clear that God expected Moses to know exactly what the Urim and Thummim were. Apparently they were objects with which Moses would have been familiar. Unfortunately, Moses did not include a description of these in the books which he wrote and we have to look for clues elsewhere.

The Hebrew words Urim and Thummim literally mean "lights" and "perfection." It is interesting that Urim begins with the Hebrew letter *aleph*, which is the first letter in the Hebrew alphabet, and Thummim begins with the letter *tau*, the last in the Hebrew alphabet. Since God is both the" beginning" and the "end," the "first" and the "last," this may have some symbolic meaning.

When the tabernacle was completed according to God's instructions to Moses and was ready for worship to begin, Moses brought Aaron and his sons to the great tent which housed the holy things of God. "And Moses brought Aaron and his sons, and washed them with water. And he put upon him the coat, and girded him about with the girdle, and clothed him with the robe, and put the ephod upon him, and he girded him with the curious girdle of the ephod, and bound it unto him therewith. And he put the breastplate upon him: also he put in the breastplate the Urim and the Thummim" (Lev. 8:6-8).

It is evident that the Urim and Thummim were separate items from the breastplate. There was either a separate fold in the breastplate or a place beneath it that was the receptacle for these objects. But what were these items and how were they used?

They had to be relatively small to fit inside the breastplate. They also were probably rather thin, for the fold of cloth of the breastplate had to accommodate both of these objects. And we may be certain that there was some difference between the two. But how were they used to determine God's will?

Again we have to look at the clues in Scripture. At the end of the 40 years of wandering in the wilderness, God would not allow Moses to enter the Promised Land. Israel needed another leader and God selected Joshua to take Moses' place and lead the people across the Jordan into Canaan. God instructed Moses to lay his hands on Joshua and put some of his own honor upon him. Then Joshua was to stand before the high priest, Eleazar, who had succeeded to this position after Aaron's death. "And he shall stand before Eleazar the priest, who shall ask counsel for him after the judgment of Urim before the Lord: at his word shall they go out, and at his word they shall come in, both he, and all the children of Israel with him, even all the congregation" (Num. 27:21).

Eleazar was to inquire of the Lord whether Joshua was to lead the people "in" or "out." This means that God would control what the Israelites did when they entered Canaan. It was perfectly clear that God himself would make the important decisions after the tribes of Israel had entered Canaan.

Joshua was to be the leader, but he was to inquire of the Lord before making any major decision. That decision was to be made through Eleazar, the high priest, who would use the Urim and Thummim to discover God's will in any important decision affecting the Israelites. It is clear that only the high priest could utilize the Urim and Thummim, for they were kept within his breastplate and the high priest was the only one who was permitted to stand before the Lord and ask for an answer.

How was this answer given? We can see from other Scripture that the question must be capable of being answered by either a yes or a no. That means that the priest must pose the question to God so that He might use the Urim and Thummim to give one of these results. It appears then that these two objects were the instruments used to cast lots to decide what the Lord desired in any situation.

The high priest might first inquire whether it was the Lord's will for Israel to attack a certain Canaanite city. The priest then might allow the Urim and Thummim to fall from their place within his breastplate. If each side were of a separate color, or contained a different marking, then how they landed might have meant a yes or a no to that question.

If the question was which of the tribes the Lord desired to lead the assault on that city, the priest might have asked, "Is it Dan?" The way in which the Urim and Thummim fell out would indicate either a yes or no. If the result was no to Dan, the priest might have asked, "Is it to be Judah?" Again the Urim and Thummim would fall from his breastplate and an answer received.

Evidence that this is how these objects were actually used may be gleaned from Scripture. After the death of Joshua, the Israelites were faced with a battle against the Canaanites. They inquired of the high priest which tribe would lead the fight. "Now after the death of Joshua it came to pass, that the children of Israel asked the Lord, saying, Who shall go up for us against the Canaanites first, to fight against them? And the Lord said, Judah shall go up: behold, I have delivered the land into his hand" (Judg. 1:1-2).

Only the high priest could make inquiry of the Lord and this was done only for the leader of Israel or to decide an important question for the nation. It was not to be used for any other inquiries concerning trivial matters. It could be used in places other than the tabernacle, the temple or where the ark of the covenant was located.[1] This is illustrated by what happened when the Israelites desired to be like the other nations and have a king. The elders of the tribes came to the old prophet Samuel with their demand. "Then all the elders of Israel gathered themselves together, and came to Samuel unto Ramah, And said unto him, Behold, thou art old, and thy sons walk not in thy ways: now make us a king to judge us like all the nations" (1 Sam. 8:4-5).

Since the Exodus, it had been God who had actually ruled over the Israelites. Through the use of the Urim and Thummim, God had communicated through the high priest His instructions. But now the people were no longer satisfied. They wished to be like their neighboring nations, and these pagan nations all had men who ruled as king over them. God was not pleased. "But the thing displeased Samuel, when they said, Give us a king to judge us. And Samuel prayed unto the Lord. And the Lord said unto Samuel, Hearken unto the voice of the people in all that they say unto thee: for they have not rejected thee, but they have rejected me, that I should not reign over them" (1 Sam. 8:6-7).

God gave the people what they asked for, but they were not aware of the consequences of their choice. God had asked nothing of the people but their obedience and worship. But a king would demand much more. Their sons would be pressed into his service, their daughters made servants, their land taken, their crops and vineyards taxed. They had not considered what they would have to pay in order to be like the neighboring, pagan nations. Israel had prospered under the theocracy of God's direct rule, now they had rejected this system of government and had demanded a monarchy, to conform to their neighboring pagan nations.

God instructed Samuel to anoint a man named Saul of the tribe of Benjamin to be the king. But in order to prove this to the elders and to all Israel, a ceremony of selection would be held and the Urim and Thummim utilized to indicate God's choice of a man.

Samuel ordered all the tribes of Israel to present themselves before him. Then the selection was made, first by tribes, then by families, then by the sons of that family. "And when Samuel had caused all the tribes of Israel to come near, the tribe of Benjamin was taken. When he had caused the tribe of Benjamin to come near by their families, the family of Matri was taken, and Saul the son of Kish was taken: and when they sought him, he could not be found. Therefore they inquired of the Lord further, if the man should yet come thither. And the Lord answered, Behold, he hath hid himself among the stuff" (1 Sam. 10:20-22).

There is no doubt that the Urim and Thummim were used to obtain God's will in the selection of the tribe, family, and eventually the man who would be king of Israel. But the final words of this Scripture have led to speculation that at times the high priest received something more than the casting of these two objects could reveal. How did the fact that Saul was hiding among the tribe's possessions come to light?

It has been suggested that at times the high priest, after praying to Yahweh for an answer, would have a thought come strongly into his mind. This would perhaps be like the revelations received from the prophets, who would then communicate to the people. To be certain that they knew it was from God and not their own words, the prophet would preface his statements by, "Thus saith the Lord."

It has also been suggested that the 12 semi-precious stones on the priest's breastplate might play a part in God's communication. Each stone was inscribed with a letter designating one of the 12 tribes. It has been proposed that as the priest prayed, these stones would somehow self-illuminate, spelling out a reply.[2]

This theory has a serious flaw, however, as not all of the letters of the Hebrew alphabet are represented in the letters engraved on the stones. Some of the replies recorded in Scripture contain such letters. This idea is also quite foreign to the methods and conceptions of Hebrew ritual.

In all probability, the Urim and Thummim were flat, rather thin stones colored differently on each side. Then, when they fell out of their pocket in the breastplate, how they landed would give three possibilities. If they were, for instance, colored white and black on opposite sides, the two objects could either land with both white sides up, both black sides up, or one white and one black side up. This is given substance by the fact that Scripture tells us that three answers could be obtained using the Urim and Thummim. A "yes," a "no," and in some instances, a non-response.[3]

After Saul had become king, he went to the high priest to inquire whether he should go and fight the Philistines and whether God would give him a victory. "And Saul asked counsel of God, Shall I go down after the Philistines? wilt thou deliver them into the hand of Israel? But he answered him not that day" (1 Sam. 14:37).

That the Lord had not answered Saul implied that there had been some grievous sin committed. Saul called the people together to find out who was responsible for this sin. Not one man would confess, so Saul had to again inquire of the Lord to find the man responsible. Saul called to his son Jonathan to stand with him, and the rest of Israel stood on the other side. "Therefore Saul said unto the Lord God of Israel, Give a perfect lot. And Saul and Jonathan were taken: but the people escaped" (1 Sam. 14:41).

The Urim and Thummim had declared that the sin had been committed by either Saul or his son Jonathan. Another inquiry had to be made of the Lord. "And Saul said, Cast lots between me and Jonathan my son. And Jonathan was taken" (1 Sam. 14:42).

When Jonathan was confronted with this, he admitted to tasting a bit of honey after his father, the king, had forbidden any of his men to eat anything until the day's battle was over. Jonathan had not heard his father issue this edict, and had dipped his rod in a honeycomb and tasted it. Since Saul had placed a curse on anyone who disobeyed his order, Jonathan must die.

The people, however, had other ideas. Jonathan had been responsible to a large extent for their military victories, and they told the king that they would not allow Jonathan's death. Saul did not continue the battle with the Philistines and they escaped back to their own land.

Eventually David was made king of Israel. But after David's reign there is no mention of the use of the Urim and Thummim. It is clear that when the Hebrews returned from exile, there was no priest with Urim and Thummim. The Book of Nehemiah tells us: "And the Tirshatha said unto them, that they should not eat of the most holy things, til there stood up a priest with Urim and Thummim" (Neh. 7:65).

The Tirshatha, a Persian title for governor, mentioned here was Nehemiah, who recognized that there was no one among the Hebrews who returned who could rightfully claim to be a Levite priest. Hence, no one could use the Urim and Thummim to inquire of the Lord.

These identical words are to be found in Ezra 2:63. In the Apocryphal book 1 Esdras 5:40 we find a similar statement. According to rabbinical tradition, the Urim and Thummim were a part of the five things which disappeared at the time of the Exile.[4]

Because Moses was apparently very familiar with the Urim and Thummim, and God did not find it necessary to explain their use to him, we can assume that the use of such objects was common before the time of the Exodus. Their names bear a strange similarity to Assyrian words which describe objects used for a similar purpose. The Assyrian *urtu* and *ertu* mean "divine decision," and this is similar to the Hebrew Urim. Thummim has been suggested to be derived from the Assyrian *tummu* with the noun *tamatu* meaning oracle.

We may never know everything about these two mysterious objects, the Urim and the Thummim, but one thing is certain. God can still direct His people in the path that He desires them to take in this world. The Bible is our roadmap to heaven, and through prayerfully seeking His direction we can be certain that God will keep us on His chosen path for our lives.

13

Solomon — Wise King or Greatest Failure?

At the mention of Solomon's name, we immediately think of wisdom and greatness and the magnificent temple that he built. But a closer examination of this man reveals something that may have been entirely different.

We say that someone who is born to great wealth and position has been born "with a silver spoon in his mouth." Solomon's spoon was not silver — it was gold — solid gold. His father, David, had forged a kingdom which extended from the Euphrates river in the north to Ezion-geber on the Red Sea in the south, and from the Mediterranean Sea to far across the Jordan River to include much of Syria, Ammon, and Edom.

David had amassed great wealth. When we estimate the gold and silver which had been stored by David for the building of the temple, and calculate its value today, it would be worth many billions of dollars.

As a young prince, Solomon would have had the best education available, with private tutors and access to the accumulated knowledge and learning of the most prominent Hebrew scholars of the day. Certainly he would have been instructed in the Law and must have been very well acquainted in the books of Moses. He would have been deprived of nothing which would have been of benefit to a future king.

Solomon's mother was Bathsheba and his father had given him a name which exemplified what David expected his son's future to entail. Solomon means "peaceful," and since David had subdued the neighboring lands and both the Egyptians and Syrians were in a militarily weakened state, he had every right to expect that Solomon's reign would be one of peace and tranquillity.

Solomon was born in Jerusalem in about 900 B.C.[1] He was probably their eldest surviving child. But David had other and older sons by other wives. In David's declining years, David's oldest son Adonijah made a strong bid for the throne, just as his brother Absolom had done years before. "Then Adonijah the son of Haggith exalted himself, saying, I will be king: and he prepared him chariots and horsemen, and fifty men to run before him" (1 Kings 1:5).

David at the time was in a coma. He had suffered from chills, and even heavy blankets could not keep him warm. As a last and desperate move to prolong his life, his servants had found a young virgin named Abishag, a Shumanite, to lay close to him in his bed to keep the dying ruler warm.

It was while David was incapacitated that Adonijah made his bid for the throne. With the support of David's deposed general, Joab, and Abiathar, the influential priest, a coronation of Adonijah was planned at En-rogel, a spring just outside of Jerusalem. For the feast of his coronation, Adonijah slew sheep and oxen and his men made ready for him to ascend to the throne of his father, David.

Adonijah invited all his brothers — except, of course Solomon — to attend. He also did not invite Nathan, the prophet, and Zadok, the priest, for he knew these men were loyal to his father. When these men heard what Adonijah had planned, they were incensed. Nathan went immediately to inform Bathsheba. "Wherefore Nathan spake unto Bathsheba the mother of Solomon, saying, Hast thou not heard that Adonijah the son of Haggith doth reign, and David our lord knoweth it not? Now therefore come, let me, I pray thee, give thee counsel, that thou mayest save thine own life, and the life of thy son Solomon" (1 Kings 1:11-12).

It was a custom of those times for a new king to immediately kill any rivals to his throne, and their families as well. Adonijah would have slain both Solomon and Bathsheba as soon as he possibly could. But Nathan was aware of a promise that David had made secretly to Bathsheba, and he urged her to act on that promise at once. "Go and get thee unto king David, and say unto him, Didst not thou, my lord, O king, swear unto thine handmaid, saying, Assuredly Solomon thy son shall reign after me, and he shall sit upon my throne? why then doth Adonijah reign? Behold, while thou yet talkest there with the king, I also will come in after thee, and confirm thy words" (1 Kings 1: 13-14).

Bathsheba did exactly as Nathan had advised her. Then Nathan entered the king's chamber and confirmed David's promise. When the king heard that Adonijah was holding his own coronation at En-rogel, he instructed Nathan to take his armed servants with him, and Zadok, the priest, and escort Solomon to the palace. They were to mount Solomon on the king's own mule and blow the trumpets as they paraded through the streets, shouting "God save King Solomon!"

They were to take the young prince to the spring at Gehon and there anoint Solomon as king of Israel. It was not long after this that David died.

Before he died, David had advised Solomon to do to Adonijah what Adonijah had planned to do to him. Adonijah was executed; Abiathar, the priest, was removed from office and banished; and Joab was slain before the altar in the tabernacle where he had fled for safety.

Now Solomon was king and there were no more threats to his throne. But it is believed that in Bathsheba, his mother, we find the first instance of a queen mother's role in placing her son upon the throne against the opposition of other wives of the king. We find that after this, the Book of Kings faithfully records the name of each king's mother.

Solomon was the first *dynastic* ruler of Israel. The judges of Israel had been chosen by God. The Lord had called His prophets to service. Saul, the first king, and Solomon's father, David, had been selected by God and anointed by God's prophets. But the hand of the Lord was upon Solomon, for while he was at Gibeon he had a vision in which God offered him his choice of gifts. Solomon asked for an understanding heart, so that he might be able to discern between good and bad and so judge his people fairly. God was apparently pleased, for Solomon received more than he had requested. "And God said unto him, Because thou hast asked this thing, and hast not asked for thyself long life; neither hast asked riches for thyself, nor hast asked the life of thine enemies; but hast asked for thyself understanding to discern judgment; Behold, I have done according to thy words: lo, I have given thee a wise and understanding heart; so that there was none like thee before thee, neither after thee shall any arise like unto thee. And I have also given thee that which thou hast not asked, both riches, and honour: so that there shalt not be any among the kings like unto thee all thy days" (1 Kings 3:11-13).

But God also said something else to the young king. "And if thou wilt walk in my ways, to keep my statues and my commandments, as thy father David did walk, then I will lengthen thy days" (1 Kings 3:14).

It was only on the condition that Solomon keep faith with God's statues, obey His ordinances, and walk according to God's ways that Solomon's days would be lengthened.

It was soon after this that Solomon's gift of understanding and wisdom was tested. Two women came before him for judgment, each claiming to be the mother of the same child. Everyone remembers what his decision was — to cut the infant into two parts and give each woman half. One woman readily agreed, but the other was horrified. She insisted that the whole child be given to the other woman. It was her reaction that allowed Solomon to determine that she was truly the child's mother, for the life of the infant was more important to her than to keep it in her possession.

Solomon became king when he was about 20 years of age. It is very likely that in the first years of his reign, Bathsheba may have played a role in the decisions that he made. One of the first of these was the marriage of Solomon to the daughter of the pharaoh of Egypt. Part of her dowry included the formerly Egyptian city of Gezer.

The work was begun on the construction of the temple. Before this time, the tabernacle had been at Gibeon and the sacred ark of the covenant was kept in Jerusalem. Because of the differences in location of the tabernacle and the ark, which was the representation of God's presence with the Hebrews, worship was not concentrated in one principle place. Many Israelites simply went up into a "high place" and built an altar. But the construction of the temple would change that, and Jerusalem would become the only focal point for worship.

It would take a huge work force to build such a structure. It was not that the building itself was that large, but the top of Mount Moriah would require considerable reconstruction. It would have to be made level and much earth and rock removed. There would also have to be timbers cut in Lebanon, and hauled all the way to Jerusalem. Since there were insufficient slave laborers for this task, Solomon had to conscript Israelites to do the work.

This was highly unpalatable to Israelites who relished their freedom. Every three months a labor force of 30,000 was taken to Lebanon to hew the wood. More Israelites were conscripted for other projects and to serve in Solomon's large army. The seeds of discontent were sown quickly among the young king's subjects.

When the construction of the temple was completed, Solomon himself led the service of consecration of God's house. His prayer at this service, unfortunately, reflected his own pride of accomplishment as much as a dedication of the house of the Lord.

Solomon also built a house for himself. This must have been extremely elaborate, for it took the workmen 14 years to complete its construction. The daughter of pharaoh must have been very demanding because Solomon had one wing of the house built just for her. It may have been that it was his Egyptian wife's influence that led to the conscription of the common people to what amounted to slave labor for Solomon's construction projects. This was what all the pharaohs did, and the poor peasants of Egypt all had to put in unpaid months each year to build the monuments, tombs, and temples of Egypt.

He did something else which greatly aggravated his subjects. From the time of the Israelite entrance into the Promised Land, when Moses divided the land among the 12 tribes, the elders of the tribes had exercised local control over their lands. Now Solomon divided Israel into 12 districts, and these were not on the boundaries of the former tribal territories. He placed a prefect in control of each district who owed allegiance solely to the king. The elders of the tribes were stripped of their power.

Solomon's lifestyle began to resemble that of an oriental potentate. He required each district to supply his royal court's requirements for one month of each year. This was not a light burden, especially for the districts with smaller populations. We learn from 1 Kings 4:22-23 that Solomon's provisions for one day was 30 measures of flour, 60 measures of meal, 10 fatted oxen and 20 ordinary ones, a hundred sheep, and an unspecified quantity of deer, wild game, and fowl.

To guard his borders, Solomon built a series of fortifications at strategic locations. David had been satisfied with foot soldiers, but Solomon was not. Pharaoh had chariots and Solomon decided that he must have an army of chariots, as well. It is estimated that he had as many as 1,400 chariots and 4,000 stalls for the horses which pulled them. The chariots he purchased from Egypt, the horses from Cilicia.[2] Since in his entire reign of 40 years, Solomon engaged in only one minor military campaign, and the neighboring nations posed no threat, the size of his army seems to be based on ego rather than need.

His chariots were based at such cities as Megiddo, Taanach, Gezer, and Hazor. Other fortified cities must also be manned with conscripted troops. The people were, of course, taxed to pay for Solomon's army.

Solomon had a unique gift for commerce. He traded not only with neighboring nations, but with such far away and exotic places as Arabia, Ethiopia, and the mystical Tarshish, which may have been the island of Sardinia.[3] He established copper mines and smelting plants for the ore. He built a seaport and shipbuilding center at Ezion-geber and the ships manned by Phoenician sailors brought back gold, silver, ivory, monkeys, and all types of exotic goods to Jerusalem.

The fabled Queen of Sheba may have come to see Solomon to discuss what could be done about commerce, for his sea routes had severely curtailed the use of overland caravans to carry trade goods from Arabia.

The Fatal Decision

It was common for men at that time to have more than one wife. It was not unusual for kings to have perhaps a dozen. Solomon's appetite for female companionship made all of the world's royal courts pale by comparison. He had decided at an early age that the best way to consolidate relations with the neighboring countries was to marry the daughters of their kings. The daughter of pharaoh was but the first of these. But Solomon, we are told, had 700 wives. Not satisfied with that, he took into his harem an additional 300 concubines. These women, it turned out, led to Solomon's spiritual downfall. "For it came to pass, when Solomon was old, that his wives turned away his heart after other gods: and his heart was not perfect with the Lord his God, as was the heart of David his father. For Solomon went after Ashthoreth the goddess of the Ziodians, and after Milcom the abomination of the Ammonites. And Solomon did evil in the sight of Lord, and went not fully after the Lord, as did David his father" (1 Kings 11:4-6).

Solomon made his first mistake in allowing his foreign wives to worship the gods of the land from which they had come. I suppose this was allowed for what might be called "diplomatic reasons," for if he had not, the women would have complained to their royal fathers and this may have caused trouble. But then, as the practice of his wives became commonplace, Solomon actually joined them in the worship of these pagan idols. But worse yet was to come. "Then did Solomon build an high place for Chemosh, the abomination of Moab, in the hill that is before Jerusalem, and for Molech, the abomination of the children of Ammon. And likewise did he for all his strange wives, which burnt incense and sacrificed unto their gods" (1 Kings 11:7-8).

Within sight of the great temple which he had built for the God of all creation to inhabit, this king who was supposed to be the wisest man who ever lived, constructed altars to the pagan gods of his foreign wives. The memory of this remains, and the hill on which this occurred is called the "Mount of Offence" to this day.[4]

God was not pleased with Solomon. In fact, the Lord had prohibited the Israelites from associating with women of these pagan lands, knowing what the spiritual outcome would most certainly be. "But king Solomon loved many strange women, together with the daughter of Pharaoh, women of the Moabites, Ammonites, Edomites, Zidonians, and Hittites; Of the nations concerning which the Lord said unto the children of Israel, Ye shall not go in to them, neither shall they come in unto you: for surely they will turn away your heart after their gods: Solomon clave unto these in love" (1 Kings 11:1-2).

What wise king, what man to whom the Lord God had given such wonderful gifts, would have deliberately ignored such a warning? Again God spoke to Solomon, but this time it was in condemnation. "Wherefore the Lord said unto Solomon, Forasmuch as this is done of thee, and thou hast not kept my covenant and my statues, which I have commanded thee, I will surely rend the kingdom from thee, and will give it to thy servant. Notwithstanding in thy days I will not do it for David thy father's sake: but I will rend it out of the hand of thy son. Howbeit I will not rend away all thy kingdom; but will give one tribe to thy son for David my servant's sake, and for Jerusalem's sake which I have chosen" (1 Kings 11:11-13).

And it happened exactly as the Lord had told Solomon. When he died at the age of 60 years — for the Lord did not extend his days — his son Rehoboam succeeded him. But just as the Lord had promised, the 10 northern tribes revolted and broke away to form a new kingdom. Solomon's son Rehoboam was left with only Judah and the city of Jerusalem — just what God had told Solomon would happen after his death.

Was Solomon truly the wisest man who ever lived? We see in 1 Kings 3:12 that God told Solomon he would be remembered for his wisdom. But he used that great gift — a free will — to exhibit great failures. He was blessed by all the advantages possible, inheriting wealth beyond comprehension, elevated to the throne of a powerful nation, having no threats of war, and being warned by God Almighty himself about what was expected of him — then threw all this away to worship the false gods of foreign women which God had already warned him against taking as wives. Solomon will be remembered as a wise man who let wisdom slip through his once-blessed fingers.

14

Who Was the Queen of Sheba?

Many legends and stories surround the mysterious queen of an exotic and wealthy country named Sheba who traveled far to visit King Solomon in Jerusalem. The stories tell of illicit romance between the two, resulting in the birth of a son who later establishes a dynastic line of rulers in Ethiopia. But all that we can be certain of concerning this woman is contained in a scant 13 verses of Scripture.

Let us look at what the Bible tells us about the queen of Sheba before we examine the legends. First we learn of the visit of this queen and where she came from. "And when the queen of Sheba heard of the fame of Solomon concerning the name of the Lord, she came to prove him with hard questions" (1 Kings 10:1).

Sheba is the ancient name for a land in what is now part of Saudi Arabia. According to ancient records, there were four groups of people who inhabited this area; the Qatabanians, the Minaeans, the Chathramthites, and the Sabaeans—who were the most important of the four groups.[1] The Sabaeans controlled the trade in frankincense, myrrh, cinnamon, and other spices. It is believed that by Solomon's time, the Sabaeans lived in the eastern area of what is now Yemen.[2]

Solomon had built a seaport on the Red Sea at Ezion-geber, and from there his ships ventured to Arabia and the coast of Africa to trade. These ships brought back gold, silver, ivory, monkeys, and peacocks; but they also returned with spices from Arabia which was the source of the Sabaean wealth.

The ships of Solomon had drastically affected the queen's income from the overland trade routes controlled by the Sabaeans. Her trip of about 1,200 miles by camel was probably prompted more by an attempt to negotiate a trade treaty than to experience for herself Solomon's highly acclaimed wisdom.

To allow her negotiations to proceed smoothly, this queen did what most oriental potentates would do. She brought gifts for Solomon, very exotic and costly bribes to incur his favor. "And she came to Jerusalem with a very great train, with camels that bare spices, and very much gold, and precious stones: and when she was come to Solomon, she communed with him of all that was in her heart" (1 Kings 10:2).

The bribes worked! She was well received by Solomon, who without a doubt was highly flattered by the visit of a queen from such a far-off country. We can imagine that the queen did not discuss the real reason for her long trip immediately. There was much flattery and small talk between them. She probably did ask him difficult questions, to further ingratiate herself with this man of supposed wisdom and great knowledge. And like other men — Solomon probably swallowed this often-used female ploy — hook, line, and sinker.

"And Solomon told her all her questions: there was not any thing hid from the king, which he told her not. And when the queen of Sheba had seen all Solomon's wisdom, and the house that he had built, And the meat of his table, and the sitting of his servants, and the attendance of his ministers, and their apparel, and his cupbearers, and his ascent by which he went up unto the house of the Lord; there was no more spirit in her. And she said to the king, It was a true report that I heard in mine own land of thy acts and of thy wisdom. Howbeit I believed not the words, until I came, and mine eyes had seen it: and, behold, the half was not told me: thy wisdom and prosperity exceedeth the fame which I heard" (1 Kings 10:3-7).

What words of flattery! No wonder Solomon was taken by this female foreign ruler. She sat listening to him expound upon the questions she asked, her adoring eyes gazing up into his. We can almost see this woman, a slight and beguiling smile upon her lips, as she appeared to hang on his every word. And when he had at last answered all of her questions, she poured out the syrup of flattery upon his willing brow, extolling his greatness and the limitless horizons of his knowledge.

But she continued: "Happy are thy men, happy are these thy servants, which stand continually before thee, and that hear thy wisdom. Blessed be the Lord thy God, which delighted in thee, to set thee on the throne of Israel: because the Lord loved Israel for ever, therefore made he thee king, to do judgment and justice" (1 Kings 10:8-9).

She really was piling on the praise now! Not only was Solomon the greatest and most intelligent man who ever lived, but God had been extremely fortunate to have such a man as Solomon to sit upon the throne of His beloved nation of Israel. Now came more bribes before she got down to the business for which she had really made this trip.

"And she gave the king an hundred and twenty talents of gold, and of spices very great store, and precious stones: there came no more such abundance of spices as these which the queen of Sheba gave to king Solomon. And the navy also of Hiram, that brought gold from Ophir, brought in from Ophir great plenty of almug trees [sandalwood], and precious stones. And the king made of the almug trees pillars for the house of the Lord, and for the king's house, harps also and psalteries for singers: there came no such almug trees, nor were seen unto this day" (1 Kings 10:10-12).

The queen could not bring all her gifts by camel, so apparently more were shipped by sea and carried aboard Hiram's ships to eventually reach Jerusalem. More gold! Precious jewels! Spices!

And great logs of sandalwood, large enough for Solomon to construct pillars for the temple — and for his own splendid personal residence — from them. These were certainly too large to have been carried all that distance on the backs of camels, so they had to be shipped by sea. Sandalwood is a hard, close-grained, light-colored, sweet-smelling heartwood of exotic Asian trees. One can picture Solomon's delight in the pillars of the temple and of his own home made from this precious wood. No other king anywhere around would have had his palace decorated with such unique pillars.

It was probably then that she got to the business at hand. We can imagine the queen, her eyes moist with tears, sobbing out to Solomon how his ships had taken away the revenue which her country had previously received from the over-land trade in spices. Couldn't some arrangement be worked out? Could not the king's great wisdom find a way to rescue her small nation from the impending doom of impoverish-ment? Of course he could! The next verse tells us that.

"And king Solomon gave unto the queen of Sheba all her desire, whatsoever she asked, beside that which Solomon gave her of his royal bounty. So she turned and went to her own country, she and her servants" (1 Kings 10:13).

Mission accomplished! The queen had gotten exactly what she had come to Jerusalem to obtain. Probably a great deal more!

The Legend of Solomon and the Queen of Sheba

There is an ancient legend in Ethiopia concerning King Solomon and the queen whom the Ethiopians claim as their own. It tells of the descendants of the Ethiopian monarchs from Solomon, king of Israel, and Queen Makeda, their name for the queen of Sheba.

That Ethiopia and Arabia could be confused is actually not that unreasonable. In fact, the Arabian peninsula and the African coast could well have been part of the same empire at one time early in history. So despite the seeming contradic-tory nations, the same queen may well have ruled both nations.

This tradition linking Ethiopian rulers to Solomon is preserved in a literary work, *Kebra Nagast (Glory of Kings)* which dates from the late thirteenth century or early four-teenth century A.D. There is evidence that the story may have existed in the sixth century A.D.

The legend begins in a decidedly mythological fash-ion, with Wainaba, the snake-dragon ruling Ethiopia. A man named Angabo mixes a poison and feeds it to his goat, then feeds the goat to the dragon — killing it. For this feat, he is made king. When Angabo dies, his daughter Makeda becomes queen.

During Makeda's reign boats arrive from Israel seeking materials with which to construct a temple. Makeda sends materials such as gold, jewels, and timber and her servants accompany the cargo, returning with great tales of Israel's king, Solomon.

Anxious to meet this great king, Queen Makeda decides to visit him herself. Solomon, according to the *Kebra Nagast* is so impressed by her beauty and intelligence that he desires to have a child by her. When her visit comes to a close, Solomon invites her to a farewell banquet and invites her to sleep with him. She refuses.

Queen Makeda asks Solomon to swear that he will not take her by force. He agrees, with a stipulation: she is not to take anything from his palace. The spicy food of the banquet makes Makeda very thirsty during the night and she asks her maid to bring her some water. The only water available is beside Solomon's bed.

Solomon awakes and seizes the maid, forcing her to sleep with him. When her maid does not return, Makeda herself enters Solomon's bedchamber to get the water. Solomon confronts the queen, accusing her of breaking her oath not to remove anything from the palace. Makeda sleeps with Solomon and the next morning Solomon gives her a ring.

During her stay in Jerusalem, Makeda has converted to Judaism and brings back this religion when she returns to Ethiopia. Both Makeda and her maid bear sons. According to legend, the maid's progeny would become Ethiopia's Zagwe dynasty.

Makeda's son, Menelik, inquires about who his father is and she informs him that it is King Solomon. She gives him the ring that Solomon had given her after their tryst and sends the boy to Jerusalem to be educated. After years of schooling at the king's court, the boy determines to return home despite Solomon's wish to make Menelik his heir to the throne of Israel.

Solomon asks his court counselors to send their own sons with Menelik when he returns to Ethiopia. The high priest's first-born son, however, is reluctant to leave the ark of the covenant behind in Jerusalem. Menelik and the priest's son make a replica of the ark to take with them. Just before they depart, the two young men conspire to switch the replica with the real ark. Thus the genuine ark of the covenant was taken by Menelik to Ethiopia where it has been ever since.

Queen Makeda receives the ark and has a temple built for it, which later becomes the church of Mary Zion in Aksum. Queen Makeda makes her son, Menelik, king. After the queen's death, Menelik is said to have a stelae erected in Aksum, and the Lion of Judah representation thus becomes the established symbol for future kings of Ethiopia.[3]

This is the legend as told in the *Kebra Nagast*. It has, however, many flaws. There is absolutely no way that the high priest, who alone was permitted to enter the Holy of Holies, would have permitted his son and Menelik to make a replica of the original ark. Also, for these two young men to have replaced the genuine ark with a hastily fashioned replica would have been utterly impossible. It is an interesting story, but it is at least an intriguing exaggeration of what may have happened.

With Solomon's certain womanizing tendencies, it is not out of the realm of possibility that he and the queen became lovers. The queen may also have borne a child by Solomon. We do not know for certain, but this is indeed a possibility. But for Menelik to have successfully carried out a plot to remove the ark of the covenant from the temple in Jerusalem is pure and simple fantasy.

But despite all of this, the queen of Sheba remains a mysterious and exotic historical figure. And I believe that for all of Solomon's supposed wisdom, he was outwitted by this queen from Arabia — who got exactly what she had come to Jerusalem to obtain.

After examining this evidence, don't you agree?

15

Hair — Its Meaning and Importance in the Bible

When Jesus reassured His disciples, and all of us, not to fear what the world could do to them, but to trust in the power of God who has the final and ultimate charge over our souls, He told them: "But the very hairs of your head are all numbered" (Matt. 10:30).

Hair was a very important thing to those in ancient times, and to us today, as well. We take good care of our hair, for it is an integral part of our appearance. The phrase "well groomed" gives a connotation of a person's hair being washed clean, combed, and brushed. Women of today are particularly interested in having hair that is attractive in appearance, but no more than women of any age.

All mammals have hair, and no species beside mammals possess it. Hair growth actually begins before birth. By the sixth month, a fetus is covered by a growth of fine hair, called the *lanugo*.

After birth, in the first few months of infancy, the *lanugo* is shed and is replaced by the hair we are more familiar with. Baby hair is more coarse over the head and eyebrows, but soft and downy over the rest of the body. At puberty, hair begins to grow more coarse on other parts of the body such as over the upper lips and lower jaw of boys as they begin to develop beards.

The rate of growth of hair varies with both age and the length of hair. When hair is cut short, it grows an average of 3/4 inch per month. If hair is allowed to grow to about one foot in length, the rate of growth is only half that of shorter hair. Hair grows fastest in women between the ages of 16 to 24 years.

Hair has a function in addition to adding to the attractiveness of an individual. The brain is susceptible to both heat and cold. A good head of hair serves to help protect the brain from temperature extremes when a person is exposed to the hot sun or bitter cold weather. A man's beard also serves to protect the sensitive skin of his face from the elements.

Hair is referred to more than 70 times in the Bible. It was not only a symbol of strength and vitality, hair played a role in a Hebrew's obedience to God.

For both men and women in Old Testament times, the normal custom appears to allow the hair of both sexes to grow to considerable length. Baldness was considered a sign of disgrace, perhaps because loss of hair frequently accompanied leprosy.

Men's Hair

It seems that the Old Testament rules regarding hair were established to set the Israelites apart from their neighbors. Egyptian men ordinarily shaved their heads and beards, although they allowed their hair to grow when in mourning.[1] The Egyptian men of rank wore wigs and false beards. The shape of these false beards were signs of rank and position. Women usually wore their hair long.

There was a practice among the idolatrous cults to allow the locks on the temples and in front of the ears to grow on the heads of young boys. Their initiation into manhood included the cutting of these locks of hair. The Hebrew prohibition against cutting the corners of their hair was apparently to set them apart from those idolaters.[2] "Ye shall not round the corners of your heads, neither shalt thou mar the corners of thy beard" (Lev. 19:27).

We still see this being observed today among some of the most Orthodox Jews who refuse to cut the lovelocks of the hair. The Bible also stated that the Israelites were not to shave their heads. "They shall not make baldness upon their head, neither shall they shave off the corner of their beard, nor make any cuttings in their flesh" (Lev. 21:5).

The Nazarites were made an exception to this. After a

Nazarite had completed his vows, he was required to shave his head. "And the Nazarite shall shave the head of his separation at the door of the tabernacle of the congregation, and shall take the hair of the head of his separation, and put it in the fire which is under the sacrifice of the peace offerings" (Num. 6:18).

But prior to that time, a razor was not to touch a Nazarite's hair. Samson was a Nazarite, and he retained his strength while his hair was not cut. He had refused to tell Delilah the secret of his great strength, but she finally prevailed upon him to reveal it. "And it came to pass, when she pressed him daily with her words, and urged him, so that his soul was vexed unto death; That he told her all his heart, and said unto her, There hath not come a razor upon mine head; for I have been a Nazarite unto God from my mother's womb: if I be shaven, then my strength will go from me, and I shall become weak, and be like any other man" (Judg. 16:16-17).

Combs are not mentioned in the Scriptures, but the Egyptians used them and it is probable that the Israelites also fashioned combs after the Exodus. The barber and his razor are, however, mentioned. "And thou, son of man, take thee a sharp knife, take thee a barber's razor, and cause it to pass upon thine head and upon thy beard: then take thee balances to weigh, and divide the hair. Thou shalt burn with fire a third part in the midst of the city, when the days of the siege are fulfilled: and thou shalt take a third part, and smite about it with a knife: and a third part thou shalt scatter in the wind; and I will draw out a sword after them" (Ezek. 5:1-2).

What God ordered Ezekiel to do in shaving his head and beard and burning the hair was to demonstrate the shame that had come to Jerusalem by military defeat. Unger writes that "The reason for this disgrace was Israel's abysmal failure in her favored position 'in the center (navel) of the nations' as a light and witness of the one true God."[3]

Absalom, the rebellious son of king David, was a handsome man whose hair grew so long that it weighed him down. Once each year he cut it. "And when he polled his head, (for it was at every year's end that he polled it: because the hair was heavy on him, therefore he polled it:) he weighed the hair of his head at two hundred shekels after the king's weight" (2 Sam. 14:26).

Josephus states that Solomon's horsemen sprinkled gold dust on their hair every day "so that their heads sparkled with the reflection of the sunbeams from the gold."[4]

Black hair was much esteemed among the Hebrews, and grey hair was considered a sign of the wisdom which should come with age. But Herod the Great preferred to look younger and not wiser. Josephus also tells us that when the king of Palestine grew old Herod dyed his hair black to make himself appear younger than his years.[5]

Women's Hair

Women generally allowed their hair to grow long. It was either bound up or braided. Light ornaments of gold or silver were worn by those who could afford them. Sometimes a tiny bell was hung on a woman's hair at the end of her tresses. Shorn hair or baldness was a disgrace for women in biblical times.[6]

When a captive or slave woman was selected as the wife of a Hebrew, her head was shaved as a sign of her purification before the marriage ceremony.[7] "And seest among the captives a beautiful woman, and hast a desire unto her, that thou wouldest have her to thy wife; Then thou shalt bring her home to thine house; and she shall shave her head, and pare her nails; And she shall put the raiment of her captivity from off her, and shall remain in thine house, and bewail her father and her mother a full month: and after that thou shalt go in unto her, and be her husband, and she shall be thy wife" (Deut. 21:11-13)

Letting loose a woman's hair was a token of her humiliation, done either by those who had caught her in an inappropriate act, or by herself as self-degradation in her repentance.

A woman's hair was her crowning glory. Paul speaks of both men's and women's hair in his first letter to the church at Corinth. "Doth not even nature itself teach you, that, if a man have long hair, it is a shame unto him? But if a woman have long hair, it is a glory to her: for her hair is given her for a covering" (1 Cor. 11:14-15).

Paul also set forth what a man and a woman should do when they pray or prophecy. "Every man praying or prophesying, having his head covered, dishonoreth his head. But every woman that prayeth or prophesieth with her head uncovered dishonoreth her head: for that is even all one as if she were shaven" (1 Cor. 11:4-5).

But Paul also warned women not to place too much attention on their hair. "In like manner also, that women adorn themselves in modest apparel, with shamefacedness and sobriety; not with braided hair, or gold, or pearls, or costly array; But (which becometh women professing godliness) with good works" (1 Tim. 2:9-10)

There appeared to be a belief among ancient people that some part of a person's life resided in that person's hair. Even today, as in ancient times, to possess a lock of a person's hair is believed to give some degree of control over that person by the witch doctor or shaman who has it in his possession. Arabs often cut a portion of a prisoner's hair before freeing him and retain it as proof that he had been in their power.

The hair was examined for any change in color due to leprosy, and if any orange or white tint was observed, it was considered a sign of that disease. The head of that person was shaved and the person put out of the community.

Signs of Grief and Mourning

As a sign of grief in many ancient cultures it was customary to cut one's hair, or even to pluck it out. Even today, it is a common Oriental custom to tear one's hair as an expression of sorrow, and Arab women sometimes cut their hair as a sign of mourning.[8]

The Bible also speaks of these customs which were practiced in biblical times. Isaiah tells of his vision when disaster is brought upon several neighboring nations. "He is gone up to Bajith, and to Dibon, the high places, to weep: Moab shall howl over Nebo, and over Medeba: on all their heads shall be baldness, and every beard cut off" (Isa. 15:2).

When Ezra found that the Hebrews who had returned from Babylonian captivity had intermarried with the pagan women, he was sorely grieved. He describes what he did when he heard this. "And when I heard this thing, I rent my garments and my mantle, and plucked off the hair of my head and of my beard, and sat down astonied" (Ezra 9:3).

We have all heard of wearing sackcloth and placing ashes on the head as a sign of sorrow, but men also at times would cut or pluck out the hair of their heads and beards. It is very evident that hair was an important symbol of a person's well-being or his emotional state.

Swearing by Hair or Beard

Hair was such an important symbol in biblical times that men even took oaths on their beards. The expressions still exist today which came from this practice. Have you ever heard anyone remark, "by my beard," or take an oath by saying, "I swear it by the hair on my sainted mother's head"? Jesus had this to say about such practices when He spoke to the multitude and delivered what we call the Sermon on the Mount. He was cautioning them about taking oaths, and swearing by heaven, or earth, or by Jerusalem, or by anything else. "Neither shalt thou swear by thy head, because thou canst not make one hair white or black" (Matt. 5:36).

Jesus warned them to let their "yea" be "yea" and their "nay" be "nay." Anything else, Jesus warned, comes from evil.

It was a sign of respect and welcome for a host to wash the feet of a guest at his home, and to anoint his guest's hair with oil. When Jesus was at the house of a Pharisee named Simon, a woman came into the house and anointed Jesus' feet. The Pharisee knew that this woman was a sinner and thought to himself that if Jesus were indeed a prophet, He would have known about this woman and would have condemned her. Jesus knew exactly what the man was thinking and rebuked him. "My head with oil thou didst not anoint: but this woman hath anointed my feet with ointment" (Luke 7:46).

Hair was important enough that even God's hair is described in Daniel's vision of Judgment Day when all must stand before His throne. "I beheld the thrones were cast down, and the Ancient of days did sit, whose garment was white as snow, and the hair of his head like the pure wool . . ." (Dan. 7:9).

The thought of that day should make your hair stand up, just as Job reported that his did. "Then a spirit passed before my face; the hair of my flesh stood up" (Job 4:15).

And this can indeed happen, your hair can actually stand up. Attached to each of your hair follicles is a minute muscle, the *arrector pili*. This muscle is under the control of the autonomic nervous system.[9] You cannot make it happen yourself, but when something very extraordinary happens, the autonomic nervous system sends a message to the *arrector pili* to contract. It is then that we humans undergo one of the strangest sensations it is possible for us to experience — our hair actually stiffens up and stands on end.

16

Biblical Weights and Measures

Take 1/2 log of shortening, add 1/4 log of oil and 1/4 kab of sugar. Stir in 1/3 omer of flour and a pinch of salt and 1/2 log of milk.

What? How much of each of these ingredients? I can understand the pinch of salt, but how much of the rest of this? What is an omer, a log, or a kab? We find these units of measurements in the Scripture, but few of us have any idea what they correspond to in our own familiar units of measurements.

Old Testament Weights and Measures

The Hebrews did not have a well-organized, systematic system of weights and measures until about the time of Solomon. Although the Bible speaks of specific units of weight and capacity, there was not an actual standard set. This resulted in quite a haphazard and approximate measurement of items during trade. Stones and scraps of metal were in common use as weights and archaeological finds indicate a significant discrepancy in them.[1]

The dishonest and greedy merchants probably fostered the continuation of such an unreliable system. The prophet Amos warns of such deceit. "Hear this, O ye that swallow up the needy, even to make the poor of the land to fail, Saying, When will the new moon be gone, that we may sell corn? and the sabbath, that we may set forth wheat, making the ephah small, and the shekel great, and falsifying the balances by deceit?" (Amos 8:4-5).

It must have been very easy to prey on the poor, who needed to sell their produce, by using a large capacity basket to measure their grain and to pay for this with silver weighed on a balance with false weights. Since coins were not used in Israel until the second temple period, silver was weighed out as payment.[2]

Micah denounced the man who cheated. "Are there yet the treasures of wickedness in the house of the wicked, and the scant measure that is abominable? Shall I count them pure with the wicked balances, and with the bag of deceitful weights?" (Mic. 6:10-11).

The shekel was the basic unit of weight. The shekel may have been originated by workers in silver and gold, jewelers by trade, because the shekel is a comparatively light unit of weight. This is suggested in the book of Job. "It cannot be gotten for gold, neither shall silver be weighed for the price thereof" (Job 28:15).

When the Bible speaks of something "priceless," the actual term used is "beyond weighing."[3] The probable first use of weighing precious metals by jewelers is suggested in Isaiah. "They lavish gold out of the bag, and weigh silver in the balance, and hire a goldsmith; and he maketh it a god: they fall down, yea, they worship" (Isa. 46:6).

The first use of the shekel as a unit of monetary weight is in the Book of Genesis when Abraham purchased land near Hebron from the Canaanite, Ephron. This field contained a cave and Abraham desired to bury his beloved wife, Sarah, there in the cave of Machpelah. "And Abraham hearkened unto Ephron; and Abraham weighed to Ephron the silver, which he had named in the audience of the sons of Heth, four hundred shekels of silver, current money with the merchant" (Gen. 23:16).

But other weights were necessary beside the shekel, because it would be necessary to weigh both large and small quantities. We find other units of measurement such as the gerah, beka, mina, and talent mentioned in the Bible.

Unit	Value	Ounces	Grams	Pounds
Talent	3,000 shekels	1,200	4,200	75
Mina	50 shekels	20	570	1.25
Shekel	—	0.4	11.4	—
Beka	1/2 shekel	0.2	5.7	—
Gerah	1/20 shekel	0.02	0.57	—

Dry and Liquid Measures

Dry materials such as grain, and liquids such as wine were measured by containers which held a specific quantity. The ephah was not only a unit of dry measurement but it also was a kind of basket.[4] In the Book of Deuteronomy, it warns against having two different sizes of baskets (ephahs) in one's house. "Thou shall not have in thine house divers measures, a great and a small" (Deut. 25:14).

The ephah is the most frequently mentioned unit of measurement of capacity in the Old Testament. It is described as holding such items as flour, barley, and grain. It was equal in volume to the bath, which is also noted in Scripture. The ephah and bath were equivalent to one-tenth of a homer.

A homer was equivalent in capacity to a kor, and both were used to measure dry and liquid materials. Other units of measurement included the seah, the hin, the omer, the kab, and the log. The relative quantities of these are given in the tables below.

Old Testament Liquid Measures

log	.56 liters	1 pints
kab (4 logs)	2.24 liters	4 pints
hin (3 kabs)	6.72 liters	4.05 quarts
bath, ephah	40.5 liters	9 gallons
homer, kor	405 liters	90 gallons

The values given in these tables are subject to debate among scholars, since verses of Scripture describing some of them are somewhat obscure. Archaeological finds have also led to differing opinions as to exact quantities assigned to Hebrew units of measurement. But the figures given in these tables are the best estimates available at this time.[5]

Old Testament Dry Measures

kab	—	2 quarts
omer	1-4/5 kabs	.9 gallons
seah	3-1/2 omers	2.7 gallons
ephah	3 seahs	8.1 gallons
lethech	5 ephahs	40.5 gallons
kor	2 lethechs	11 bushels
homer	2 lethechs	11 bushels

Since our cookbooks tell us that 2 cups equal one pint, we can see that in our Hebrew recipe, we would have to mix together 1 cup of shortening, 1/2 cup of oil, 2 cups of sugar, and stir in 5-1/2 cups of flour, 1 cup of milk, and a pinch of salt. The pinch of salt, of course, would be the same no matter in what culture, time, or place we might be doing the cooking.

Measurement of Distance

It is certainly not surprising that men who lived several thousand years before the birth of Christ used the most commonly available tools to measure distance. The width of a workman's finger or the span of his hand were always handy — and he could never forget to take them with him on a job.

The standard measure of length, the cubit, was the distance from a man's elbow to the tip of his middle finger. Of course, the bigger the man, the longer the cubit, but on average this seemed to work out fairly well until a king, probably a pharaoh of Egypt, decided to standardize the cubit by making a metal rod the length of his own forearm from which other standard rods could be calibrated. But access to this standard measure was difficult and the cubit remained by and large a measurement of the individual workman's forearm.

Other readily accessible units of length were the width of a finger, the palm of the hand, and the span which was the distance between the little finger and the thumb when the fingers were spread. For longer distances, the workman would use other innovative methods of marking off lengths. Tall reeds were handy, so that he would cut one of these to a length equal to six times the length of his forearm. Not surprisingly, this was called a "reed."

For longer distances, a workman would count the number of strides it took to walk the measurement. Each step should be of equal length, about twice that of his forearm. The pace therefore was equivalent to two cubits. For distances between villages, a larger unit of measurement was required. The *stadium*, or furlong, and the *milion*, or mile, came into use to measure greater distances, although these were very probably calculated by how many paces it took a man to walk the distance between the two points.

Almost all ancient people began measuring distances by comparison with the forearm's length. In Genesis, we find that God gives Noah the dimensions of the ark in this term. Moses was also given the specifications for the tabernacle in cubits. All through the Bible we find reference to this unit of measurement. But how much did a cubit measure in terms we are familiar with?

Take a ruler and measure the length of your own arm, from the tip of the elbow to the tip of your extended middle finger. You will probably find that this is just short of 18 inches. We can estimate from archaeology, how long a cubit was in biblical times. The tunnel which was constructed in Jerusalem by Hezekiah to bring in water from the Pool of Siloam is 1,749 feet long. There is an inscription which states that it measured 1,200 cubits. This would give a cubit of 17.49 inches. This figure compares quite well with what we know about the common cubit used in Egypt.

Kings are proud people, and this can be demonstrated in unusual ways. Apparently kings in biblical times were not satisfied to have their buildings and tombs constructed with the common cubit as a basis of measurement. Hence, there came into existence the royal cubit. Apparently some of the kings of Israel followed the custom of Egyptian royalty and established their own royal cubit. Both the Egyptian and Hebrew royal cubit was about 20.7 inches.

The following table indicates units of measurements used and the best information concerning what they are in modern measurements.

Unit	Royal System		Common System	
	Meters	Inches	Meters	Inches
Finger's breadth	0.022	0.86	0.019	0.74
Palm = 4 fingers	0.088	3.44	0.075	2.95
Span = 3 palms	0.262	10.33	0.225	8.86
Cubit = 2 spans	0.525	20.7	0.450	17.72
Reed = 6 cubits	3.150	124.0	2.700	106.3
Pace = 2 cubits			3 feet	
Fathom = 2 paces			6 feet	
Plethron = 10 reeds			90 feet	
Stadium, or furlong = 200 paces			600 feet	
Milion, or mile = 1,500 paces			4,500 feet	

The Sabbath Day's Journey

Jews were forbidden to perform any work on the Sabbath, including cooking and the usual chores. But they could walk a certain distance to attend religious ceremonies. Since this distance was not actually prescribed by God, it fell to the priests to set the maximum distance a Jew could travel on the Sabbath without breaking the fourth commandment. How did the priests solve the question of how far a person might walk on the Sabbath?

The priests looked for some precedent, some distance, which might give them a clue to what God would allow in this situation. And they found such a clue. When the Israelites followed the ark of the covenant, they kept behind it at a distance of 2,000 cubits. Since Jews had been allowed to attend worship at the ark during the 40 years of wandering in the wilderness, this must be the distance that God would allow on the Sabbath.

Since 2,000 cubits was equal to 1,000 paces, each Jew must count out the number of paces he walked and keep it at or below a thousand. In our units of measurement today, this would be 3,500 feet, or a little over a half of a mile. The Mount of Olives is just about this distance from Jerusalem, and Jesus walked this distance on the Sabbath.

There is evidence which indicates that in later times the distance allowed on the Sabbath was increased to 3,000 cubits, and this is noted in the Talmud. Some Jewish sects such as the Zadokites limited the Sabbath's days journey to 1,000 cubits.[6]

New Testament Weights and Measures

The first miracle that Jesus performed was at the wedding feast at Cana where He changed the water into wine. The water was contained in stone waterpots. "And there were set there six waterpots of stone, after the manner of the purifying of the Jews, containing two or three firkins apiece" (John 2:6).

The Greek word *metretas*, measures, has been translated here as "firkins." The stone containers would have contained 20 to 30 gallons of water each. The six waterpots would have held between 120 and 180 gallons. That must have been an extremely large wedding, or those celebrating it were feeling no pain after consuming that much wine.

In Matthew 5:15, Jesus says that people do not place a lamp under a bushel. The word *modios* used here in the Greek means bushel, or a basket used as a unit of measurement. This would correspond to about 1.7 gallons. The pots referred to in Mark 7:4 held one *xestai*, or just over one pint.

The Roman mile or *milion* referred to in Matthew 15:41 was 4,854 feet, or about 9 percent shorter than the English mile of 5,280 feet.

In John 12:3 we are told that Mary used a *litra*, or pound of costly ointment of spikenard to anoint Jesus' feet. In John 19:39 Nicodemus brought a hundred pounds of myrrh and aloes to prepare Jesus' body for burial. Again the Greek word *litra* is used which corresponded to about 12 ounces.[7]

In New Testament times the actual weights and measures for various units could vary considerably, as they had for centuries, according to the geographical area and the specific period of time. And although the Bible admonishes merchants to use just scales and honest weights, then as always, the buyer had to beware.

Money in Biblical Times

Jesus praised the poor widow who put all of her money into the temple treasury. We are told that this was two "mites." Jesus also called for a coin to be brought for Him to see when the Scribes and Pharisees sought to trick Him by asking whether it was lawful to pay tribute to Caesar. They brought out what was called a "penny." What were these coins and how much were they worth — in those times — and today?

Then there is the most infamous price placed on a life, the 30 pieces of silver that Judas Iscariot was paid for betraying Jesus to the high priest and led to His death on the Cross. How much money was this? What was the price placed on the head of the Son of God?

Barter, the exchange of one type of goods for another, was the original method of trade and this continued to be the prime method of business even after the introduction of various weights of metals as money. In fact, the Latin word for cattle, *pecus*, became the Latin word for money, *pecunia*. This indicates that at one time cattle were the principal standard of value. Indeed, in many cultures even today, the number of cattle a man owns is indicative of his wealth.

Money was not coined until about the eighth century B.C. and the first coins were probably introduced in Asia Minor by the Lydians and Greeks.[8] Herodotus writes that the Lydians were the first to issue coins. Staters, minted from electrum, an alloy of gold and silver, were struck in Lydia and silver coins in Aegina as early as 700 B.C.[9]

Even then, the people of most of the biblical world, including Palestine and Egypt, were content to use gold and silver objects such as bars, rings, and other objects as the medium of exchange. In some cases these might be stamped with a seal attesting to their weight or value, but these were not issued by any civil authority.

The Hebrews did not mint their own coins until Simon Maccabeus was briefly granted this right in 140 B.C.

John Hyrcanus issued small copper coins and Herod the Great and his successors did the same, but it was primarily Greek coins which circulated in Palestine prior to Roman times and continued to be legal tender even after the Roman denarius came into common usage.

When Abraham paid 400 shekels of silver to Ephon for the field which had a cave in which to bury Sarah, he did not count out that amount in coins. The silver was weighed out on a balance to settle this business arrangement. Since the shekel was a weight equal to 0.4 ounces, the cost of the burial site for Sarah was 160 ounces of silver. At the current price of silver, Abraham would have paid about $900 for the field.

We are told that David, after he had provided all of the gold, silver, brass, iron, wood, and precious stones for the temple, gave of his own fortune the gold and silver to overlay the walls of this sanctuary. "Even three thousand talents of gold, of the gold of Ophir, and seven thousand talents of refined silver, to overlay the walls of the house withal" (1 Chron. 29:4).

The talent was equivalent to 1,200 ounces, so David gave 3,000 X 1,200 ounces, or 3,600,000 ounces of gold. At today's value, the gold would be worth almost one and a half *billion* dollars. The 7,000 talents of silver would be worth about 42 million dollars at today's prices.

After the temple had been constructed by Solomon, the

land of Israel prospered greatly. In addition to other income, Solomon received enormous amounts of gold. "Now the weight of gold that came to Solomon in one year was six hundred threescore and six talents of gold" (1 Kings 10:14).

This amounted to a yearly income of over 300 million dollars in gold at today's value. When the tremendously increased purchasing power of gold and silver in those times are considered, Solomon must have indeed been the wealthiest man who ever lived. As an example of this, consider the price of the field that Jeremiah bought. "And I bought the field of Hanameel my uncle's son, that was in Anathoth, and weighed him the money, even seventeen shekels of silver" (Jer. 32:9).

At today's value for silver, Jeremiah only paid about $40 for this field. But money in those days purchased considerably more than money of today. The apocryphal book of Tobit informs us of one drachma a day being offered as wages.[10] This was the equivalent of about 74 cents. The working day was from dawn to sunset, or about 12 hours. Today, at minimum wage, a person would earn about $55 for a day's labor of 12 hours. You can readily see what the difference in purchasing power was for money in those times.

In the time of Jesus, one Roman denarius, worth about 20 cents, was the rate of pay for a day's labor. A Roman soldier's pay was two and a half sesterces a day in the latter days of the Roman republic. This was the equivalent of one and a quarter denarii, and the soldier was expected to pay for his clothing, weapons and tent out of this meager daily wage.[11]

The denarius, the "penny" of the Bible, was the coin which Jesus asked to see when the Scribes and Pharisees attempted to trick him into committing treason when they asked if it was lawful to pay tribute (taxes) to Caesar. The denarius was inscribed with a relief of the emperor's head and his name. Since this coin was struck by Caesar and bore his image and name, Jesus told them that it belonged to Caesar, not God. "And Jesus answering said unto them, Render to Caesar the things that are Caesar's, and to God, the things that are God's . . ." (Mark 12:17).

It was also the denarius which was used when two coins were given by the good Samaritan to the innkeeper to take care of the man who had been beaten and robbed.

The coins which the widow placed in the treasury when Jesus said that she had given more than all those who had made contributions to the temple that day is translated as two "mites." These were leptons, the smallest copper coin in circulation in Palestine, and each was worth about one-eighth of a cent.[12] It is apparent that the size of the gift is not important to the Lord, but the sacrifice that the gift represents, for we are told that it was all of the money that the poor widow possessed.

The widow's mite, the Hebrew lepton, was temple money. The priests would not accept any foreign coins, for this would profane the treasury of the temple. Of course, this provided an excellent source of income, for those who did not possess Hebrew coins were forced to exchange their foreign coins for acceptable ones by doing business with the moneychangers. There always was a certain amount of this transaction held back by the moneychanger as the fee for the exchange.

This business was transacted in the Court of the Gentiles, and it was from this area of the temple complex that Jesus smashed the stalls and drove off the merchants whose business was in changing foreign coins into more acceptable ones.

Business was exceptionally good for the moneychangers when each year Jewish law required every male Jew, 20 years of age or older, to pay half a shekel into the treasury. Since most of the coins in circulation in Palestine were either Greek or Roman, the moneychangers made considerable profit from the feast day.

The reason given for most coins profaning the temple was that both Greek and Roman coins contained what the priests considered to be heathen symbols. The Tyrian coins did not contain these symbols and these and the few local Hebrew coins that were sometimes available were the approved temple money.

Even the doves, lambs, and other animals for sale in the Court of the Gentiles must be purchased with temple money. Not only were exorbitant prices charged the worshippers, but they also had to exchange their coins with proper ones to pay for their sacrifices. Jesus was furious when He saw how His Father's house had been turned from a house of prayer into a den of thieves.

But the most infamous account of the use of money occurred the same night as the Last Supper. Judas betrayed Jesus and his payment was 30 pieces of silver. How much, we might ask, was the life of God's only begotten Son worth in earthly money to those who sought to kill Him — and the man who agreed to betray Him?

Judas Iscariot was paid 30 denarii for delivering Jesus into the hands of the high priest and ultimately His death on Calvary. From the time of Augustus Caesar to Nero, the denarius was fixed at a standard weight of 60 grains of silver.[13] The 30 denarii were the equivalent of a month's pay for a soldier or a common laborer. It was also the going price for a slave in those times.

How much would this have been in our times? The life of Jesus Christ cannot be measured in monetary terms. How can man place a value on the life of the Son of God? But we can compute the value of those 30 pieces of silver in relation to what silver sells for on today's market. Jesus Christ, the Son of Almighty God, was sold by Judas Iscariot for the paltry sum of $22.20 worth of shiny metal.

How much is He worth to You?

17

Pharisees, Sadducees, and Essenes — What Did They Believe?

In the New Testament there are two religious sects that are mentioned — the Pharisees and the Sadducees. We know that there was at least one other sect, the Essenes, that were in existence at that time, but they are not referred to in the Scriptures. We also see that there were men who were scribes.

Jesus seemed to have nothing good to say about either the Pharisees, Sadducees, or the scribes. In fact, it appears that both Jesus and John the Baptist held both sects in utter contempt. John was baptizing at the Jordan when he looked up and saw many of the Pharisees and Sadducees come to see what he was doing. "But when he saw many of the Pharisees and Sadducees come to his baptism, he said unto them, O generation of vipers, who hath warned you to flee from the wrath to come? Bring forth therefore fruits meet for repentance. And think not to say within yourselves, We have Abraham to our father: for I say unto you, that God is able of these stones to raise up children unto Abraham" (Matt. 3:7-9).

Jesus was equally as harsh in His condemnation. In the temple they all had tried to trick Jesus into saying something which could be considered treason against Rome. After likening them to whitewashed tombs, beautiful on the outside but inside full of corruption, He shouted at them: "Ye serpents, ye generation of vipers, how can ye escape the damnation of hell?" (Matt. 23:33).

Were these supposedly religious men all that bad? And were all of the Pharisees, Sadducees, and scribes evil men? What is the origin of these separate Jewish sects? What did they believe? And what happened to them? We will attempt to answer these questions briefly in this chapter.

The Pharisees

It is very probable that the sect of the Pharisees had roots in the time of Ezra, about 450 B.C. The Jews had returned from their exile in Babylon and by that time it is estimated that 50,000 Jews were living in towns chiefly around the city of Jerusalem.[1]

Artaxerxes was king of Persia and the land of the Jews was under his direct control. When Cyrus had allowed the Jews to return, he had not allowed them to rebuild the walls of the city, and the inhabitants were under attack by the Samaritans who resented their return. The Jews attempted to build up the walls as protection and the Samaritans appealed to the king to prevent this, telling Artaxerxes that a strong Jerusalem would pose a danger to his already weakening empire.

They sent the king a letter which is quoted in the Book of Ezra: "Be it known unto the king, that the Jews which came up from thee to us are come unto Jerusalem, building the rebellious and the bad city, and have set up the walls thereof, and joined the foundations. Be it known now unto the king, that, if this city be builded, and the walls set up again, then will they not pay toll, tribute, and custom, and so thou shalt endamage the revenue of the kings" (Ezra 4:12-13).

They asked the king to have the records searched, to determine whether or not the Jews had caused trouble in the past. The king's men searched the old records and indeed found that in past history the Jews had made several insurrections against authority. Artaxerxes ordered that the work be stopped immediately.

Despite his order against building a walled city, Artaxerxes looked with favor upon the request of Ezra to return to Jerusalem to rebuild the temple and to teach the Jews the law of God. Funds were provided by the king for Ezra's mission, for the king knew that the loyalty of the Jews was essential for his continued authority over the neighboring lands of Syria and Egypt.

When Ezra returned to Jerusalem, he was faced with a major problem. Many of the Jews had intermarried with non-Jews. He knew that in the past this had led to a corruption of their belief in God and their eventual return to idolatry. This had to be dealt with before anything else could be accomplished.

Ezra pleaded with his people to remain pure and to follow to the letter the law of Moses. If they did not, he expected God to pour out His wrath again, and perhaps this time there would be no remnant to return from another exile. The Jews as a nation might well cease to exist.

Ezra's words were heeded. Those who had intermarried agreed to put away their foreign wives and the children which had resulted from such marriages. A divorce court was established to decide each case and the list of the divorces among the priests was added to the end of the Book of Ezra.

Then Ezra set out to teach others to master the Law. Those whose lives became dedicated to this work and attempted to carry out the Law meticulously were the first of the *hasidim*, meaning "God's loyal ones." These Hasidaeans searched out all of the surviving copies of the old books they could locate, and they made additional copies of them. Hence, the Hasidaeans were the first scribes, and the scribes of the New Testament were their spiritual descendants.

The first mention of the name "Pharisee" appears at the time of the early Hasmonaean priest-kings. Apparently there was a decline in the rigorous following of the Law and a dispute over whether the king should also be the chief priest. There was a split among the Hasidaeans and a small minority withdrew and awaited intervention by God, who had promised to send the "Anointed One." These were the first Pharisees and the name means "the separated ones." The goal of those Hasidaeans who remained was the control of the religion of the state.

The Pharisees who separated themselves did not go into isolation. Rather they lived in the smaller villages and towns among the common people. In fact, it was the popularity of the Pharisees among the people which gave John Hyrcanus (134-104 B.C.) his base of power. Because of this, the Pharisees had considerable influence initially with this Hasmonaean ruler.

When the Pharisees became dissatisfied with Hyrcanus' leadership, they broke with him and he turned to the Sadducees for support.[2] Later, in the reign of Alexander Jannaeus (103-76 B.C.), their opposition to the Hasmonaeans went so far as to appeal for help to the Seleucid king of Syria, Demetrius III. Jannaeus had 800 of his leading opponents put to death by crucifixion.[3] Apparently his arrangement with the Sadducees did not turn out the way he expected, for on his deathbed Jannaeus advised his wife, Alexandra Salome (76-67 B.C.), to turn over the government to the Pharisees when she succeeded him.

For a time the Pharisees held a dominant position in the Sanhedrin, but when they suffered under Antipater and Herod the Great, they apparently realized that politics could not bring about a spiritual change in the lives of people. The Pharisees petitioned Rome for direct rule by Roman administrators. This was accomplished in A.D. 6 when Archelaus was removed as tetrarch by Augustus Caesar.

Although the Gospels mention the Pharisees frequently, they were always a minority group. In the time of Jesus they numbered only about 6,000.[4] Their initial closeness with the common people eroded as they began to interpret the passages of the Talmud more stringently, relying on oral traditions and past interpretations taken sometimes to an extreme degree.

The poor people, who had to constantly struggle to put food on their family table, had little interest in the strict and sometimes harsh and legalistic attitude of the Pharisees. The Gospels also indicate that although they interpreted the Law stringently for others, many of them violated the spirit of the Law in practice. Jesus told the people that unless their righteousness exceeded that of the Pharisees, they could not enter the kingdom of heaven.

The Pharisees were not priests. Many of them were of the poor or middle classes of society. But these men were the self-appointed scholars of their time, and they felt that their own interpretations of the Law, as modified by the oral tradition passed down as the *Mishnah*, was the true and only correct guide to living.

They believed strongly in education. The first schools

were begun by Pharisees several centuries before the birth of Christ. Only boys were to be educated. The primary classes were held in what was called "the house of the book." At five years of age, a boy began reading the Scriptures. At 10, he would study the Mishnah and its interpretations of the Law. For those showing aptitude, higher education was held in "the house of study."

Classes were taught by a rabbi, usually a lay Pharisee. Some schools became famous and attracted students from far and wide because of the teacher. The school of the Jewish teacher Shammai was noted for extremely conservative interpretations while the school of Hillel was more liberal in its views.

The apostle Paul in his youth was a student at the school taught by Gamaliel, the grandson of Hillel. Each student was expected to also learn a trade so that he could earn his own living and not be a burden on others. Paul, as you remember, was a tentmaker and worked at this trade to support himself through much of his ministry.

In spite of the criticism of Jesus of the Pharisees of His time, the Pharisees for the most part tried their best to do what was right for their people. Certainly, without them, Jewish boys would have grown up by and large illiterate. It was the Pharisees who held onto the Law through hard times and frequent attempts to force Jews to become "Semitic Greeks." The Pharisees of the time of Jesus had many faults, but they had in the past been of great service to their people.

What the Pharisees Believed

The Pharisees believed that it was an individual's duty to keep the Mosaic Law as well as the nation's duty. It was Israel's failure to keep these laws, they believed, which led to the Babylonian captivity. But the Pharisees also held in high regard the oral tradition, and held that the commandments were not all "fixed" but were adaptable to conditions that changed from time to time. They believed that they, as students of the Law, had the responsibility of teaching the people what and when these changes were to be implemented and that their decision was binding upon all Jews.

The Pharisees believed that the soul was immortal and would be reunited with the body in the Resurrection. They believed in angels, devils, and the physical place of hell where those who did not share their strict interpretations of the Law were certain to spend eternity.

Pharisees were strict advocates of the tithe. Not only was their monetary income subject to the tithe, but all that they grew, including as Jesus said, mint and herbs. But He called them hypocrites for the manner in which they conducted themselves. "But woe unto you, Pharisees! for ye tithe mint and rue and all manner of herbs, and pass over judgment and the love of God: these ought ye to have done, and not to leave the other undone" (Luke 11:42).

By the time of Jesus, the Pharisees had degenerated into something far different than they had previously been. Now they laid the heavy burdens of their legal interpretations of the oral law upon the common people, but they held high opinions of their own righteousness. They sought out the acclaim of men and desired the best seats at dinners and other functions.

God had instructed the Israelites to wear blue fringes on their robes to indicate their commitment to God's Law. Even Jesus would have worn one on His garment. But the Pharisees wore large fringes on their robes to boast that their personal dedication exceeded others. They wore larger than normal phylacteries on their foreheads and on their left arms to morning prayers, again as a false show of great piety.

They refused to eat in the home of a non-Jew, nor would they purchase any food from him in case the food had first been offered to idols. They insisted on personal cleanliness, washing their hands frequently.

But the beliefs of the Pharisees had little to do with theology. Its roots lay in personal ethical behavior. We must bear in mind as we read of Jesus' condemnation of the Pharisees, that these men were the most ethical of all the Jews in Palestine.

The Sadducees

Unlike the Pharisees, the Sadducees rejected the oral traditions and concentrated on the Torah, the first five books of the Old Testament. They came primarily from the wealthy and upper classes of Hebrew society and almost all were priests. The emphasis of the Sadducees was on temple worship.

It is not known exactly when this sect was formed but they were definitely in existence during the time of John Hyrcanus (134-104 B.C.). Their name may have been derived from the Hebrew word *saddig,* meaning "righteousness."[5] Some scholars believe that the name comes from the name of Zadok, since the Sadducees concentrated on temple worship.[6]

There was a marked difference in philosophy between the Sadducees and the Pharisees. The Sadducees readily accepted the Hellenistic outlook and adopted the beliefs of the Greek philosopher Epicuris, who taught that the soul dies with the body.[7] They loved debates about matters of philosophy and theology. These men scorned the interests of the common people and had little support from them.

The Pharisees opposed the high priesthood of John Hycanus because of a false story that his mother had been raped during the reign of terror instigated by Antiochus IV.[8] Under the Pharisidic interpretation of the oral law, this act against his mother would have "defiled" John Hycanus and he would not be eligible for the high priesthood. When John Hyrcanus proved in court that the story had been concocted by an enemy, the Pharisidic court punished the man convicted of lying with only a few lashes. Hyrcanus was incensed and he withdrew his support for the Pharisees and turned instead to the Sadducees.

When Hyrcanus died there was a battle between his sons for leadership, eventually won by Alexander Janneus. He had studied Greek under tutors in Rome and was sympathetic to the position of the Sadducees until an incident during the Feast of Tabernacles when he was pelted by an unruly crowd who opposed him. Alexander ordered his soldiers to attack the crowd and they killed 6,000 people.[9]

The Pharisees, who were now the champions of the common people, waged a civil war against Alexander which ended when he captured and crucified 800 Pharisaic leaders. As Alexander was dying, he advised his daughter to again place the government in the hands of the Pharisees, but neither they nor the Sadducees were to forget this bloody period of strife between themselves.

Later during the reign of Herod, magnificent sports arenas were constructed where Greek-style games were held.

The Pharisees were opposed to such events but the games were enthusiastically supported by the Sadducees.

The Sadducees believed that each man had control over his own destiny and that God played no part in a man's private life. Man was to perform the obligatory worship at the temple, but what he did outside of that was up to the individual.

They were rude and argumentative, rather boorish men from wealthy, priestly families. Their number was probably no greater than the Pharisees, but they had much greater political influence. Even when they held power, because they lacked the support of the common people, the Sadducees were often forced to make political alliances with the sect of Pharisees.

What the Sadducees Believed

Sadducees held that this life was all there was to existence, there was neither reward nor punishment for how a person lived it, and that man had the free choice between good and evil. They believed that prosperity or adversity were the outcomes of that choice.

They were masters of accommodation and compromise. Since their land was ruled by foreign powers, they readily adopted the lifestyle of their conquerors.

They rejected any notion that God interferes in the course of events. Man, they held, was in full control of his fate on earth. They denied the validity of the oral traditions held in high esteem by the Pharisees, contending that only the written laws contained in the Pentateuch were to be regarded.

They did not believe in either angels or demons. They contended that life was to be enjoyed to the fullest and that if men lived according to the laws of the Torah, they would enjoy wealth and a good life. If men did not obey the laws of the Torah, they would face hardship and poverty. Since they came from the wealthiest families of Palestine, the fact that they were well off was sufficient to prove that they lived proper lives.

Since the entire theology of the Sadducees revolved around temple worship, the destruction of the great temple built by Herod in A.D. 70 by the Romans effectively ended this sect. With the temple gone, there could no longer be animal sacrifices made, for this was allowed only on the altar of the Jerusalem temple. No temple meant no further need for priests and the sect of the Sadducees vanished.

The Pharisees taught in the local synagogues and had established schools for the education of Jewish young men. The destruction of the temple, although a great blow to Judaism as a whole, did not mean the end for the Pharisees. Their lay teachers had been called rabbi by the people as a term of respect. This term was to be later applied to the Jewish clergy and the rabbis of today are really the descendants of the Pharisees of biblical times.

The Essenes

Of the three major sects which existed in Palestine, we know less about the Essenes than the other two. In fact, we are not certain that these men even called themselves by that name. In any event, they most probably also emerged from the movement known as the *Hasidim*.[10]

Several writers of that time mention the Essenes but they give us scant information about them. Josephus writes that there were two groups of Essenes.[11] But Hippolytus writes in his *Refutation of All Heresies* that there were four.

The most detailed description of Essene life, if it is accurate, comes from the writings of Pliny. But since he lived after the destruction of Jerusalem, his work is probably dependent on accounts written earlier by others such as Alexander Polyhistor in the first century B.C. Pliny describes Essene life in his writing about the Dead Sea and says that the Essenes lived on the west side north of En Gedi. This agrees with the discovery of what is believed to be an Essene settlement at Quamran.

Pliny writes that they have lived there for countless generations, living apart from society and renouncing both women and money. Their numbers are sustained, even increased, from men who have become dissatisfied with life in Palestine joining their order.[12]

Philo of Alexandria (20 B.C. - A.D. 50) also wrote about the Essenes.

There is a portion of those people (Jews) called Essenes, in number something more than four thousand in my opinion, who derive their name from their piety, though not according to any accurate form of the Grecian dialect, because they are above all men devoted to the service of God, not sacrificing animals, but studying rather to preserve their own minds in a state of holiness and purity. These men, in the first place, live in villages, avoiding all cities on account of the habitual lawlessness of those who inhabit them . . . these men, some cultivating the earth, and others devoting themselves to those arts which are the result of peace, benefit both themselves and all those who come in contact with them, not storing up treasures of silver and gold, nor acquiring vast sections of the earth out of a desire for ample revenues. . . . Among those men you will find no makers of arrows, or javelins, or swords, or helmets or breastplates, or shields; no makers of arms or military engines; no one, in short, no one attending to any employment whatever connected with war . . . there is not one slave among them, but they are all free . . . no one has a house absolutely his own property, that it does not in some sense also belong to every one . . . all their expenses are in common . . . their garments belong to them all in common . . . their food is in common . . . those who are sick are not neglected because they are unable to contribute to the common stock . . . and yet no one, not even of those immoderately cruel tyrants, nor of the more treacherous and hypocritical oppressors was ever able to bring any real accusation against the multitude of those called Essenes or Holy. . . .[13]

From Josephus we get a detailed account of the initiation procedure required for new members of this sect. There was a three-year probation period. At the end of the first year the novice was admitted to the ritual purification in water, but it was not until he had successfully passed the requirements during the next two years that he could share the common meal with full-fledged brothers. At the end of the three-year probation, the candidate was required to swear a succession of solemn oaths.

Daily life began before sunrise and, according to Hippolytus, "They continue in prayer from early dawn and speak no word until they have sung a hymn of praise to God."[14]

It is remarkable that we know so little about the Essenes, for some of them apparently lived in Jerusalem. There was a gate to the city called "The Essenes' Gate." From the Dead Sea Scrolls, we can surmise that the Essenes believed themselves to be guardians of "mysterious truths" which would come to light when the Messiah came to govern Israel. They wrote of war being waged between the forces of darkness and the forces of light.

They apparently also meticulously copied books of the Old Testament. In the caves at Quamran, either whole or partial manuscripts have been found of all Old Testament books with the exception of Esther.

What the Essenes Believed

It is difficult to ascertain just what the Essenes believed, and it will not be until the translation of more of the Dead Sea scrolls that this will become clear. They certainly lived strict moral and ethical lives. They apparently obeyed the law of Moses. And it is certain that the Essenes were "Messianic," for their central theme was the imminent coming of the Anointed One, promised by God in the Scriptures. Other than this, we cannot with accuracy tell what the Essenes believed. We will have to wait and read more of what they, themselves, had to say about their beliefs as the Dead Sea scrolls become available to us.

Some scholars believe that it was among the Essenes that John the Baptist spent his early manhood. It is peculiar that John described himself as the one who "makes straight the way of the Lord" and this is apparently a central theme in some Essene writings. It is surprising that Jesus does not mention the Essenes, for He certainly was aware of them. But perhaps it was His omission of them in His condemnation of the Pharisees and Sadducees which is much more important.

The Scribes

Scribes were scholars, experts in the law of Moses. Initially all scribes were priests and the offices were not necessarily separate. Ezra was both a priest and a scribe. "And

Nehemiah, which is the Tirshatha, and Ezra the priest the scribe, and the Levites that taught the people, said unto all the people, This day is holy unto the Lord your God . . ." (Neh. 8:9).

Nehemiah was the "Tirshatha," which was a title given by the king of Persia to him meaning "governor," and Ezra was both a priest and a scribe. The primary activity of a scribe was the study of the law. Although there may have been scribes prior to the Babylonian exile, they came into prominence after the return to Judaea.

It is believed that the scribes were the originators of service in the synagogue. Since scribes were professional students of the law, it was the scribes who taught the young boys in the synagogues and lectured in the temple. They were referred to as "lawyers" and "teachers of the law." Actually, the words "scribe" and "lawyer" are synonymous and are never used together in the New Testament. Scribes probably also served as judges in the administration of the law in the Sanhedrin.

It is believed that the scribes were not a political party at first, but because of the oppression under Antiochus Epiphanes, became one and banded together for protection.[15]

Some scribes were probably members of the Sanhedrin. "Then assembled together the chief priests, and the scribes, and the elders of the people, unto the palace of the high priest, who was called Caiaphas, And consulted that they might take Jesus by subtlety, and kill him" (Matt. 26:3-4).

Scribes were closely associated with the Pharisees and perhaps many scribes also were Pharisees. But as a body, they were a distinct entity. When Jesus condemned the scribes and Pharisees for transgressing the commandment of God, teaching as doctrine the commandments of men, He was referring to the work of the scribes who believed that the oral tradition was superior to the written law contained in the Torah.

In the oral law, the scribes had determined that the Torah contained 613 commandments. Of these, 248 were positive and 365 were negative.[16] To insure that no one would break any one of these 613 "commandments" by either accident or ignorance, the Scribes then proceeded "to make a hedge" about the Law.

This was accomplished by placing in the oral tradition so

many stipulations concerning what a Jew could or could not do that it would be impossible for anyone not to observe all 613 of the commandments of the Law. Jesus inferred that in doing this, the letter of the Law might be observed but that they had ignored the spirit of the Law.

What the Scribes Believed

The Scribes thought of themselves as guardians of the Law. In theology, Scribes were generally in agreement with what the Pharisees believed and no doubt most Scribes were also members of that sect. They sided with Paul against the Sadducees on the matter of the resurrection of the body (Acts 23:9).

They opposed Jesus, for He taught with authority and the people stopped listening to the Scribes to follow the "unlearned" man from Nazareth. They were jealous and conspired with the Sadducees and Pharisees to rid themselves of this man who was dangerous to their position. They participated in the death of Stephen (Acts 6:12). But among the Scribes were some who believed (Matt. 8:19). Nicodemus may have been a scribe as well as a Pharisee.

What we see among the religious leaders of biblical times is fairly representative of religion today. We find a wide divergence of position in Palestine in the time of Jesus Christ, with both liberal and conservative parties of Jews attempting to influence their followers and to dictate the course of government. It is not difficult to find parallels of the Pharisees, Sadducees, Essenes, and Scribes in the panorama of Christian theology of today.

I am certain that when Jesus returns, He will have something to say about all of these.

18

The Two Messiahs of the Bible — Why the Jews Missed Jesus!

The Jews living at the time of Jesus had ample warning that He would be born. The Scriptures of the Old Testament were full of prophecy concerning the coming of the Messiah. They even gave the place and circumstances of His birth. There were over 100 messianic prophecies in the writings available to them at that time. Daniel even gave the exact year that He would come. The Scribes, the scholars who studied the Torah and the writings of the prophets, were experts in this field. Yet, when Jesus of Nazareth came, most of the Jews who should have recognized Him as the Messiah, did not. Why? How could so many Jews have missed Him?

To understand how this could have happened, we must first look at the prophecies concerning the coming of the Anointed One, the Saviour whom God had promised to send to His people. When we are aware of what they say, perhaps we can better understand why the Jews missed Jesus.

The Place, Time, and Circumstances

There should have been no doubt in the minds of those who studied the Scriptures where the Messiah would be born. This was written down very plainly for all to see and know by the prophet Micah. "But thou, Bethlehem Ephratah, though thou be little among the thousands of Judah, yet out of thee shall he come forth unto me that is to be ruler in Israel; whose goings forth have been from of old, from everlasting" (Mic. 5:2).

From this passage of Scripture, there could be no doubt

in anyone's mind that the Messiah was to be born in the small town of Bethlehem in Judea. When this is compared with other prophecies that the Messiah would be of the lineage of the great king, David, it should have been seen as fitting that He would be born in the city of David.

We know that the Scribes were well aware of this. When the kings from the east, the magi, came to inquire where the new king of the Jews could be found, they told Herod of the prophecy that it would be at Bethlehem where the Messiah would be born.

That the Messiah would be born of a virgin had also been foretold. About 800 years before, Isaiah had written of the virgin birth. "Therefore the Lord himself shall give you a sign; Behold, a virgin shall conceive, and bear a son, and shall call his name Immanuel" (Isa. 7:14).

When writing of this Redeemer who would come to Zion, Isaiah also told about the magi coming to pay homage to the Messiah at His birth. "And the Gentiles shall come to thy light, and kings to the brightness of thy rising" (Isa. 60:3).

The kings of the East followed the brightness of His star to Jerusalem, where they met Herod. He did not know what they were talking about and called for the chief priests and the scribes. "When Herod the king had heard these things, he was troubled, and all Jerusalem with him. And when he had gathered all the chief priests and scribes of the people together, he demanded of them where Christ should be born. And they said unto him, In Bethlehem of Judaea: for thus it was written by the prophet" (Matt. 2:3-5).

Herod was furious. He was the king of the Jews and would allow no chance for this new born child to threaten his throne. When the kings were warned in a dream not to return to Jerusalem and tell Herod where the child was, he decided to eliminate the possibility of a rival. He ordered the death of all male Hebrew children of the age of two years and younger in Bethlehem.

God had known exactly what the evil king, Herod, would do. In fact, the massacre of these innocent children had been prophesied by Jeremiah over 500 years before. "Thus saith the Lord; A voice was heard in Ramah, lamentation, and weeping; Rahel weeping for her children refused to be comforted for her children, because they were not" (Jer. 31:15).

The Rahel here refers to Rachel, who was the wife of Jacob. She died when her second son, Benjamin, was born and was buried near Bethlehem. Rachel's tomb may still be seen just outside the town and Hebrew women who have been barren come here to pray, believing that their prayers will be answered and that they will conceive children.

Joseph also had a dream. In it he was warned that Herod would try to destroy the young child. He took Mary and the child and fled into Egypt. Later, after Herod had died and his equally evil son, Archelous, had been removed from power in Judea, the Lord told Joseph in a dream that it was safe for them to return.

Again, this had been prophesied hundreds of years before. "When Israel was a child, then I loved him, and called my son out of Egypt" (Hos. 11:1).

It is understandable that the birth of Jesus could have been missed. A poor and insignificant couple from the backwoods town of Nazareth had happened to be in Bethlehem to pay their taxes and be counted in the census. Their arrival and departure had attracted no attention. It was only when the shepherds were confronted by the Lord's host that night and were told of the birth of Jesus that anyone had been aware of it.

Then the rich kings had come. Surely they would have been seen coming to the cave behind the inn. Men of their status would not have gone unnoticed. And the shepherds had certainly told others what they had experienced. But when all of the Hebrew children were slain by Herod's men, the people would have been too frightened to talk very much about this baby who had been born in a stable. A stable was, after all, not the place where a king would be expected to be born.

When the ministry of this strange young man from Nazareth began, those who studied Scripture would have had another sign by which He should have been recognized. There was to be another man who would go before him. Isaiah had foretold of the one preparing the way for the Messiah. John, who baptized in the Jordan, attracted considerable attention. "The voice of him that crieth in the wilderness, Prepare ye the way of the Lord, make straight in the desert a highway for our God" (Isa. 40:3).

Isaiah was not the only prophet to write about this man who would come before the Messiah. Malachi also did. "Behold, I will send my messenger, and he shall prepare the way before me: and the Lord, whom ye seek, shall suddenly come to his temple, even the messenger of the covenant, whom ye delight in: behold, he shall come, saith the Lord of hosts" (Mal. 3:1).

Many of the people thought that John was the Messiah. John was quick to deny that he was. Instead, he quoted the Scriptures when he told them: "I indeed baptize you with water unto repentance: but he that cometh after me is mightier than I, whose shoes I am not worthy to bear: he shall baptize you with the Holy Ghost, and with fire" (Matt. 3:11).

It would seem to me that the Scribes and Pharisees, who knew the Scriptures concerning the Messiah, would have stayed close to John to see who he indicated the real Messiah would be. If they suspected John of being the Anointed One, then at least their interest had been aroused. But John insulted them, calling them vipers and hypocrites. They were so furious with John that they would have killed him if they were not afraid of what the people would then do to them.

Even the time of the coming of the Messiah had been prophesied. It was Daniel, writing over 500 years before, who had given the exact date. "Know therefore and understand, that from the going forth of the commandment to restore and to build Jerusalem unto the Messiah the Prince shall be seven weeks, and threescore and two weeks: the street shall be built again, and the wall, even in troublous times" (Dan. 9:25).

The Scribes and priests knew that the "weeks" in Daniel's prophecy meant "weeks of years." What Daniel was telling them was that 483 years after the commandment went out to restore Jerusalem, including the street and the wall, the long-awaited Messiah would come to His people.

Daniel wrote this during the captivity in Babylon. Nebuchadnezzar had destroyed the city of Jerusalem and the magnificent temple that Solomon had constructed. Daniel had also prophesied that the captivity would last for 70 years before the Jews would be allowed to return to Judea.

In 539 B.C. the Babylonian empire fell to the Persians. In the year 538 B.C., the Persian king Cyrus allowed the Hebrews to return to their homeland. The amazing thing about this particular event is that it was foretold by Isaiah almost 200 years before. Isaiah's prophecy is even more amazing in that it actually gives the name of the Persian king who will free the Hebrews. It tells of the rebuilding of the city of Jerusalem — even though at the time that Isaiah wrote it — the city and temple were still standing in all its splendor. This is what Isaiah wrote: "That saith of Cyrus, He is my shepherd, and shall perform all my pleasure: even saying to Jerusalem, Thou shalt be built; and to the temple, Thy foundation shall be laid" (Isa. 44:28).

It is very probable that the Hebrew scholars began to count the years from the year that Cyrus allowed the captives in Babylon to return. The king had even furnished money and materials with which to rebuild the temple. Certainly, the Messiah would come to them 483 years after Cyrus had issued this order.

But they had ignored the "fine print" of Daniel's prophecy. Cyrus had not allowed the Jews to rebuild the walls of the city. He wanted no fortified towns which could serve as bastions of rebellion against him. Cyrus' commandment had not fulfilled all of Daniel's prophecy. It had left out one important ingredient — the walls being rebuilt.

It was not until Nehemiah obtained permission from another Persian king, Artaxerxes, to build the walls of the city, that the real countdown could begin. This was in about 450 B.C. (we cannot be absolutely certain of the year). But if we count out the 483 years from this date, we arrive at A.D. 33 when Jesus was crucified and arose from the dead — fulfilling to the letter every one of the messianic prophecies.

Many scholars had expected the Messiah to come in about 55 B.C. When that did not happen, those who came after them may have lost confidence in Daniel's prophecy. But those who looked for the Him to appear in 55 B.C. had neglected to take all aspects of the prophecy into account. Daniel was perfectly accurate, even to the building of the wall in troublesome times.

The Samaritans under Sanballat, resentful that the Judeans would not allow them to participate in the rebuilding of the temple, were warring with the residents of Jerusalem. The wall had to be constructed with workmen holding a tool in one hand and a weapon in the other.

But there was something else which puzzled the Scribes as they poured over the Messianic prophecies. There seemed to be *two* separate and distinct Messiahs described in prophecy. How, they reasoned, could that be true?

The Triumphant King

About one-third of the prophecy described a victorious and powerful King. He would come into the city of Jerusalem triumphantly, and the people would greet His arrival with happiness. "Rejoice greatly, O daughter of Zion; shout, O daughter of Jerusalem: behold, thy King cometh unto thee: he is just, and having salvation; lowly, and riding upon an ass, and upon a colt the foal of an ass" (Zech. 9:9).

The King would enter Jerusalem in triumph! But what was the extent of this King's kingdom? "For unto us a child is born, unto us a son is given: and the government shall be upon his shoulder: and his name shall be called Wonderful, Counsellor, The mighty God, The everlasting Father, The Prince of Peace. Of the increase of his government and peace there shall be no end, upon the throne of David, and upon his kingdom, to order it, and to establish it with judgment and with justice from henceforth even for ever. The zeal of the Lord of hosts will perform this" (Isa. 9:6-7).

This prophecy left no doubt about the King, the Messiah that God had promised to send. He would have all power and His dominion would last forever. He would defeat the enemies of Israel, which at that time was the mighty Roman empire which occupied their land.

Daniel had also written about this King. "And there was given him dominion, and glory, and a kingdom, that all people, nations, and languages, should serve him: his dominion is an everlasting dominion, which shall not pass away, and his kingdom that which shall not be destroyed" (Dan. 7:14).

What was that? All nations, all languages, all people would serve the King of Israel, the Messiah, when He came to claim His kingdom! That would make Israel the most important, the wealthiest, the most prestigious nation in all the world! What a wonderful King this Messiah would be!

And this King would not be a tyrant. No more would a man like that Idumean Herod rule over them. This King would be one of them! He would be from the lineage of the great King David. "In those days, and at that time, will I cause the Branch of righteousness to grow up unto David; and he shall execute judgment and righteousness in the land" (Jer. 33:15).

From these and other prophecies in the Scripture, there was no doubt that the Messiah would be a great King, a mighty warrior who would subdue all of Israel's enemies and make the nation again the most powerful and prosperous in the world. They dreamed of the glory days of Solomon all over again when Messiah came to drive out the Roman and take control of the government.

But there were other prophesies, disturbing ones. These did not portray a powerful King at all. In fact, they described someone entirely different. In the idiom of today, this Messiah would be a wimp and a loser! The scribes were at a loss to reconcile the prophesies into a single Messiah. So there must be two Messiahs!

The Suffering Messiah

When the Scribes read what Isaiah wrote about the Messiah, they could not believe that this could possibly be the great and conquering King that other Messianic passages described. "He is despised and rejected of men; a man of sorrows, and acquainted with grief: and we hid as it were our faces from him; he was despised, and we esteemed him not. Surely he hath borne our griefs, and carried our sorrows: yet we did esteem him stricken, smitten of God, and afflicted. But he was wounded for our transgressions, he was bruised for our iniquities: the chastisement of our peace was upon him; and with his stripes we are healed" (Isa. 53:3-5).

What kind of King was this? Certainly it could not be the same one that the other Messianic scriptures depict!

But Isaiah had more to say about this man. "He was taken from prison and from judgment: and who shall declare his generation? for he was cut off out of the land of the living: for the transgressions of my people was he stricken. And he made his grave with the wicked, and with the rich in his death; because he had done no violence, neither was any deceit in his mouth" (Isa. 53:8-9).

The Messiah was cut off out of the land of the living? He

was *killed?* What sort of great and powerful King would allow himself to be slain? Surely, this could not be the same King of other Messianic prophecy!

And then they read that he would be betrayed, and sold for a price. "Yea, mine own familiar friend, in whom I trusted, which did eat of my bread, hath lifted up his heel against me" (Ps. 41:9). "And I said unto them, If ye think good, give me my price; and if not, forbear. So they weighed for my price thirty pieces of silver" (Zech. 11:12).

This Messiah was to be despised? Shamed? His throne cast down? And the Messiah would be put to death! God forbid! "Thou hast made his glory to cease, and cast his throne down to the ground. The days of his youth hast thou shortened: thou hast covered him with shame . . ." (Ps. 89:44-45).

There was more. In other Scripture they read that this Messiah would be mocked and insulted. His followers would desert Him. And He would be crucified!

The gory details of His death were written in Scripture. He would be given vinegar to drink as He thirsted. Those who would kill Him would cast lots for His garments. His side would be pierced but none of His bones would be broken. But He would be beaten unmercifully, so bad that the features of His face would be almost unrecognizable.

There was no way that this could be the King who was to come and make Israel the most powerful nation in the world! This was not the one who would restore to this land the glory that it had enjoyed under Solomon. This had to be an entirely different person.

There was only one solution to this perplexing problem: There must be *two* Messiahs. Why, they did not know, but it was clear that the Scripture pictured two entirely different men. There was the Messiah who was to be despised and rejected — a man whose life would be full of sorrow and misery, and eventually be killed. Then there was the powerful King who would destroy the enemies of Israel and establish this land in its former place of prominence and prosperity. That was it! There would be two separate Messiahs!

Why They Missed Jesus

The Sadducees, who were the ruling religious party at the time, rejected any concept of a Messiah. This life was all there was. The soul did not survive death. They were well off now, having compromised what little faith they formerly had, and were eager to maintain their comfortable lifestyle. They did not want some pretender to come along claiming to be the Messiah. That would bring trouble to Rome and that was the last thing the Sadducees wanted. To them, there was no such thing as a Messiah.

The scribes might well have been looking for two separate and distinct Messiahs, the mighty King and the lowly and suffering man of sorrows, but their eyes were open to only one of these. They had enough trouble with the Romans. The only Messiah they were looking for was one powerful enough to set them free from Roman rule.

They had miscalculated the starting year of the countdown for Daniel's prophecy concerning the appearance of the Messiah. That time had long since gone and he had not come. The Sadducees were content with the status quo, they had learned to live with Roman rule — and prosper with it. The Pharisees still longed for the glory days of the past, as did the majority of the common people. What they were looking for was someone to improve their earthly status. They were very content with the condition of their souls.

Then along came this itinerant preacher from the backwoods. And this upstart had the audacity to insult them to their faces, calling them hypocrites — and worse. And to make matters even more intolerable, the common people flocked to hear Him. Imagine, the people had turned away from them to hear this troublemaker talk about religion. After all, they were the experts in the field of religion, not this unlearned and untutored former carpenter from Nazareth, of all places.

Something had to be done. This man, Jesus, had to be silenced. For all they knew, with the crowds that He was attracting there might even be a revolt against the Romans. They were certain to lose, but who knew what disaster that might bring. What the Pharisees, scribes, and Sadducees had built up under Roman rule could be wiped out in a flash if the people were to rebel against Rome.

This man, Jesus, was certainly not the powerful Messiah who would restore the glory of the past. All this man could do is bring trouble down on their heads. He must be silenced. He must be killed. There was no way that this man from Naza-reth could be the Messiah, no matter what kind of miracles He might be able to perform. He must be some sort of magician, in league with Satan, to do the things He was reported to have done. He certainly was not of God, or He would have recognized the excellent lives they lived, and their good work in preserving the law of Moses.

They all, for their own reasons, missed the greatest event in Jewish history. Except for the poor, common people who had heard Him speak and had believed, only a few of the elite, such as Nicodemus and Joseph of Arimathaea recognized Jesus as the long-awaited Messiah.

The Scribes who looked for two Messiahs were actually correct. What they did not understand was that the two were to be the same person. When Jesus came to earth the first time, born of lowly circumstances, He was the man of sorrows that they read about. The prophecy came true. Jesus fulfilled each and every one of the over 100 individual prophecies concerning the Messiah. On His last day of life, Jesus fulfilled 31 separate messianic prophesies. Three days later, when He arose from the dead, He fulfilled the last of them. "For thou wilt not leave my soul in hell; neither wilt thou suffer thine Holy One to see corruption" (Ps. 16:10).

The Kingly Messiah

When Jesus arose from the dead at the Resurrection, He fulfilled all of the prophecies concerning the sorrowful Messiah. Now all the prophecy concerns the mighty and powerful King who will rule all nations, and to whom every knee will bow. Jesus is reigning now from the right hand of God, the Father. The Kingdom is already His, for He has already defeated Satan. All that remains now is for Him to return to physically claim His throne.

At the Second Coming, we will not see the "man of sorrows." No one will abuse Him again, and none will reject Him. When Jesus returns, it will be in the glory and majesty of the greatest King in the universe. The prophecy concerning the kingly Messiah will soon be fulfilled. Get ready to greet your King.

19

Where and When Did Baptism Originate?

As Christians, we tend to think that we invented baptism. Indeed, the first mention of this act in the Bible is John the Baptist immersing people in the Jordan as a sign of their repentance. "Then went out to him Jerusalem, and all Judaea, and all the region round about Jordan, And were baptized of him in Jordan, confessing their sins" (Matt. 3:5-6).

John knew who he was and what his mission was to be. John was the voice crying in the wilderness: "For this is he that was spoken of by the prophet Esaias, saying, The voice of one crying in the wilderness, Prepare ye the way of the Lord, make his paths straight" (Matt. 3:3).

And soon the One for whom John was preparing the way came, and Jesus went to the Jordan where John was baptizing. "Then cometh Jesus from Galilee to Jordan unto John, to be baptized of him. But John forbad him, saying, I have need to be baptized of thee, and comest thou to me? And Jesus answering said unto him, Suffer it to be so now: for thus it becometh us to fulfil all righteousness. Then he suffered him" (Matt. 3:13-15).

John knew about baptism and considered it a part of repentance. Jesus, who needed no repentance, thought it so important that He be baptized that He insisted that John baptize Him. From this we can see that the immersion of a person in water did not begin with Christians, but was practiced long before the time of Jesus by the Jews.

Neither John nor Jesus was preaching anything tremendously unusual when they spoke of the necessity of the believer to be baptized. Jews not only practiced ritual cleansing through a rite which parallels baptism, but during the time between the Testaments it was one of the rites necessary for proselytes converting to Judaism.[1]

Under Jewish custom, not all water was suitable for baptism or ritual cleansing. The water had to be "flowing" or "living." Water that was drawn from a cistern was considered impure and not suitable. As long as people were near the Jordan or another river or a gushing spring, this was no problem. But when the location had no running water from a stream, river, or spring there was a way to get around the stipulated requirement of "flowing" water.

The answer is stipulated in the *Mishna*, a code of Jewish laws which states how to circumvent this problem. "Flowing" water, it explains, purifies "drawn" water. For instance, if a pool of collected rainwater was connected by a conduit to the *mikveh*, the Hebrew word for the place where the immersion would take place, water could be drawn from a cistern to almost fill the *mikveh*. Then water was allowed to flow from the pool of rainwater into the *mikveh*. The addition of this "flowing" water would then purify the drawn water from the cistern and make all of the water suitable. Archaeologists have found numerous *mikvehs* in the ruins scattered all over Israel. From these we can determine something about the ritual itself. Since the person entering the *mikveh* is ritually unclean, that person would pollute any steps used to gain access to the bath. Hence, two separate series of steps are usually found in the ruins of a *mikveh*, one for entrance to the bath and another for the exit.[2]

Complete immersion was required in the bath. Mainmonides wrote, "Whosoever immerses himself must immerse his whole body, naked and all at once.... And if any who is unclean immerses himself in his garments, the immersion still avails him since the water enters through the garments and these do not interpose."[3]

A witness was required for this ritual cleansing, but it was not necessary for this to be a rabbi. This was carried over into Christian baptism, for the disciples were not rabbis. Originally total immersion was practiced, but later in the history of the church other forms of baptism are recorded.

Affusion, the pouring of water over the person being baptized was accepted. Finally the practice of aspersion, the sprinkling of water on the person's head was also considered acceptable. Doctrinal splits among various churches over the validity of total immersion versus sprinkling have occurred.

The Jews who lived in the settlement at Quamran, believed to be Essenes, had very stringent rules regarding ritual cleansing. This was considered a required purification, especially after a person had "defiled himself" by contact with a corpse, having sexual intercourse, nocturnal emission, or having a physical impairment.[4]

Women were considered unclean after giving birth to a child and ritual cleansing was necessary for them.[5] A woman was also unclean after her monthly menstrual period. After being cleansed in water, the person still had to wait until sundown to be considered clean. Even the hair must be immersed and a women who entered the ritual bath with a ribbon in her hair invalidated the cleansing.[6]

Ritual cleansing was necessary at Jerusalem before offering a sacrifice in the temple. When Paul brought several young men with him to Jerusalem to deliver the gifts from the churches to the Jerusalem Christians, they went into the ritual bath for purification. Some Jews who had known him in Asia saw them. "Then Paul took the men, and the next day purifying himself with them entered into the temple, to signify the accomplishment of the days of purification, until that an offering should be offered for every one of them. And when the seven days were almost ended, the Jews which were of Asia, when they saw him in the temple, stirred up all the people, and laid hands on him, Crying out, Men of Israel, help: This is the man, that teacheth all men every where against the people, and the law, and this place: and further brought Greeks also into the temple, and hath polluted this holy place" (Acts 21:26-28).

Excavations near the Temple Mount have uncovered a number of *mikveh*. Adjacent to where the two large staircases led up to the Temple Mount, a number of these have been found. They were apparently to serve the large number of Jews who came to Jerusalem during the three pilgrimage festivals of Pesach (Passover), Shavot (Weeks), and Sukkot (Tabernacles). It was probably in one of these that Paul and his friends had purified themselves in preparation for entering the Temple.

This type of bathing was not to remove dirt from the participants, for they were required to wash their feet and bodies prior to entering the *mikveh*. Immersion in the water of the ritual bath was spiritual in nature, supposedly cleansing that person from the sins that he had repented of prior to bathing.

The Christian Baptism

Our word "baptize" is derived from the Greek *baptizo*, meaning to immerse, to go under, or to sink. Although this may describe the physical act of Christian baptism, it does not begin to convey the spiritual meaning of this to the believer.

When Nicodemus came to inquire of Jesus by night, secretly for he was a Pharisee, he was told something that he could not then comprehend. ". . . Verily, verily, I say unto thee, Except a man be born again, he cannot see the kingdom of God" (John 3:3).

Nicodemus shook his head in bewilderment. ". . . How can a man be born when he is old? can he enter the second time into his mother's womb, and be born? Jesus answered, Verily, verily, I say unto thee, Except a man be born of water and of the Spirit, he cannot enter into the kingdom of God" (John 3:4-5).

Being born again, Jesus told Nicodemus, involves baptism. A person must be born of both the water and the Spirit before that person may enter the kingdom of God. The immersion into the water symbolizes death to this world. Rising up from the baptismal water represents resurrection. Death and resurrection is equivalent to that person being "born again." Paul expressed this perfectly: "Know ye not, that so many of us as were baptized into Jesus Christ were baptized into his death? Therefore we are buried with him by baptism into death: that like as Christ was raised up from the dead by the glory of the Father, even so we should walk in newness of life" (Rom. 6:3-4).

This newness of life that Paul speaks of is ourselves, after we have been "born again" into new creatures. And when we have been "born again" in this life, we have the promise of something far greater. Again Paul tells us what that is. "For if we have been planted together in the likeness of his death, we shall be also in the likeness of his resurrection. Knowing this, that our old man is crucified with him, that the body of sin might be destroyed, that henceforth we should not serve sin" (Rom. 6:5-6).

For the Christian, baptism is being crucified with Christ. We are dead to our old ways of sin, walking in a new spirit. Again Paul gives us a promise of greater things to come. "For he that is dead is freed from sin. Now if we be dead with Christ, we believe that we shall also live with him: Knowing that Christ being raised from the dead dieth no more; death hath no more dominion over him. For in that he died, he died unto sin once: but in that he liveth, he liveth unto God. Likewise reckon ye also yourselves to be dead indeed unto sin, but alive unto God through Jesus Christ our Lord" (Rom. 6:7-11).

Jesus Christ is the Living Water, the only water that can wash us so completely clean that we are new persons, "born again" into a new life. Through our dying in the water of baptism, we symbolize death to our old selves and sinful past. We are clean because we have been washed clean by the blood of His death.

And when we emerge from that baptismal water, all our past has been drowned by God, as thrown into the "sea of forgetfulness." We are forgiven, and by having died once, need not fear dying again, for we are His.

Old Testament Foreshadows of Christian Baptism

When the sea was parted in the Exodus, the Israelites passed through the waters to free themselves from Egyptian slavery. Since the Bible uses Egypt to typify sin, and they passed through the water to free themselves from the Egyptian bondage, they were foreshadowing the Christian baptism which signifies the washing away of sin.

The Jordan River was parted at the end of their 40 years of wandering in the wilderness. It is perhaps not by accident that the Bible tells us that the Israelites actually spent some of that time in a place named "the wilderness of Sin." "And the took their journey from Elim, and all the congregation of the children of Israel came into the wilderness of Sin, which is between Elim and Sinai, on the fifteenth day of the second month after their departing out of the land of Egypt" (Exod. 16:1).

Apparently the Israelites had not left their sin behind when they had left Egypt, even though they had passed through the waters of cleansing. They were hungry and thirsty and instead of being thankful for their deliverance, they blamed Moses for their current situation. "And the whole congregation of the children of Israel murmured against Moses and Aaron in the wilderness" (Exod. 16:2).

They were in need of another "baptism" and this was to come 40 years later. When Joshua led them into the Promised Land, the ark of the covenant was carried to the banks of the rain swollen Jordan River. As the feet of the Levites who carried the ark touched the water, it parted to leave a pathway of dry ground.

This time, as the children of Israel passed through the water, they emerged in a new land, the one which God had promised to give to them as descendants of Abraham. In a sense, we as Christians enter a new land — a promised land — as we emerge from the baptismal water. As born-again children of God, we become members of the kingdom of God. And as Jesus preached that the kingdom of God was at hand while He still walked the earth, we enter into this Kingdom when we are baptized.

The parting of the waters of the Exodus and those of the Jordan were foreshadows of things to come. And just as Joshua led the Israelites through the waters of Jordan into a new and better land, another Joshua (Jesus in the Greek) was to lead all who would believe in Him through the waters of repentance into the glorious kingdom of His Father.

If you are not a full-fledged citizen of this Kingdom, don't wait another moment. Apply for citizenship immediately. Tomorrow may be too late.

20

Who Was the Eavesdropper in Gethsemane?

In three of the Gospels, there exists an enigma which has puzzled Bible scholars as long as the New Testament books have been available to them. On the night of the Last Supper, Jesus had taken His disciples to the Garden of Gethsemane. Judas Iscariot had left the house where they had eaten and had gone to betray Jesus. The Lord left all but three of the remaining disciples and had taken Peter, James, and John with Him a short distance away to pray. "And he went a little further, and fell on his face, and prayed, saying, O my Father, if it be possible, let this cup pass from me: nevertheless not as I will, but as thou wilt" (Matt. 26:39).

After Jesus had prayed, He returned to find Peter, James, and John fast asleep. He admonished Peter: "And he cometh unto the disciples, and findeth them asleep, and saith unto Peter, What, could ye not watch with me one hour?" (Matt. 26:40).

Jesus went away the second time. Again He prayed: ". . . O my Father, if this cup may not pass away from me, except I drink it, thy will be done" (Matt. 26:42).

Again Jesus returned to find the three disciples asleep. He left them sleeping and went away a third time to pray, saying the same words. Returning again to His disciples, He said: ". . . Sleep on now, and take your rest: behold, the hour is at hand, and the Son of man is betrayed into the hands of sinners" (Matt. 26:45).

Then Jesus must have seen the men coming across the valley from Jerusalem. Judas was leading the temple guards to where they would be able to seize Jesus. There was no more time for the disciples to sleep. "Rise, let us be going: behold, he is at hand that doth betray me" (Matt. 26:46).

This scene in the Garden of Gethsemane is repeated almost word for word in the Gospels of Mark and Luke. The enigma is this: If the disciples Jesus took with Him to pray had all fallen asleep, then who heard Jesus say what is recorded in these three Gospels? Who was the eavesdropper who overheard Jesus say these words?

To try to solve this puzzle, we must go back to where Jesus and His disciples had come from when they went to the Garden of Gethsemane. It was the house in which they had eaten the meal we call the Last Supper. Whose house was this?

We are told of the ownership of only one house in Jerusalem where this could have been held. The disciples were all from Galilee. They probably knew no one personally who lived in this city. When Jesus sent them into Jerusalem to find a suitable place to eat the meal we call the Last Supper, He instructed them to look for a man carrying a pitcher of water and to follow him to his house where there would be an upper room.

It would seem a strange thing to look for, a man carrying a pitcher of water from a well, but to the disciples it meant a very unusual man, for carrying water was strictly women's work and men seldom were to be seen carrying a pitcher.

They did this and Jesus followed them there later with the other disciples. That evening, after they had left this house, Jesus was betrayed by Judas and seized to stand trial. Only a few days later, after the climactic days of the trial and crucifixion, the disciples were staying at a house in Jerusalem when the two Marys came to tell them that the tomb was empty.

A short time later we are told the identifying feature of this house. After Jesus ascended into the clouds from the Mount of Olives, they returned there. "Then returned they unto Jerusalem from the mount called Olivet, which is from Jerusalem a sabbath day's journey. And when they were come in, they went into an upper room, where abode both Peter, and James, and John, and Andrew, Phillip, and Thomas, Bartholomew, and Matthew, James the son of Alphaeus, and Simon Zelotes, and Judas the brother of James" (Acts 1:12-13).

All 11 of the disciples lived in the upper room of this house. But in the house were others. "These all continued with one accord in prayer and supplication, with the women, and Mary the mother of Jesus, and with his brethren" (Acts 1:14).

Whose house was this? I believe that we are given the answer later in the Book of Acts. Peter had been cast into prison and the disciples expected him to be executed. But an angel appeared and released Peter and his chains fell off and the gates of the prison opened of their own accord. Peter knew of only one place to return to in order to find the rest of the faithful. "And when he had considered the thing, he came to the house of Mary the mother of John, whose surname was Mark; where many were gathered together praying" (Acts 12:12).

We have now established that Mark's mother, whose name was Mary, owned the house with the upper room that the disciples used as their own home while they were in Jerusalem. But we are given another relationship which brings us closer to solving the puzzle of the young man who eavesdropped that night in the Garden of Gethsemane.

Paul wrote a letter from Rome to the Colossian Church. At the end of this epistle, he sends greetings from those who are in Rome with him. One of these men was Aristarchus, and the other was John Mark, who had been with him and Barnabas on his first missionary trip. "Aristarchus my fellowprisoner saluteth you, and Marcus, sister's son to Barnabas, (touching whom ye received commandments: if he come unto you, receive him)" (Col. 4:10).

So now we have information that Barnabas was the brother of Mary, the mother of John Mark, and it was in Mary's house that the disciples lived while they were in Jerusalem. It was also highly probable that it was in this house that Jesus and the disciples ate the Last Supper. Barnabas was likely the man carrying the pitcher of water. But who was the eavesdropper?

John Mark was only a young boy at this time. Years later, when his uncle Barnabas and Paul began their first missionary trip, Mark was allowed to accompany them. But Mark was still a very young man at this time. Later Mark was to serve as Peter's secretary for about 12 years and with Paul for several years in Rome.

He would have been hardly more than a child or teenage boy at the time of the Christ's crucifixion. But if it was his mother's house where the Last Supper was eaten, and his uncle Barnabas had been the man whom the disciples followed home, then Mark would have been in this house when Jesus offered the wine and bread to the 11 as representing His blood and body. When they left to return to the Garden of Gethsemane, the young John Mark could well have followed them.

In John Mark's Gospel, something is revealed which appears in no other of the books. It is something that only John Mark would have known. When Jesus was taken by the guards from the temple, His disciples ran away. There was no one left but Judas Iscariot and the men who had come to arrest Jesus remaining at Gethsemane. No one, that is, but the eavesdropper who had followed them from the house to this place. And only this eavesdropper could have known what John Mark wrote about him. "And they all forsook him, and fled. And there followed him a certain young man, having a linen cloth cast about his naked body; and the young men laid hold on him: And he left the linen cloth, and fled from them naked" (Mark 14:50-52).

Who else but the young man to whom this happened would have known about it? And who else but this young man could have heard the words of Jesus, as He prayed while Peter, James, and John were asleep? No one but John Mark fits as the missing piece of the puzzle. I believe that the same John Mark, who wrote the first of the Gospels, was the eavesdropper who overheard the prayers of Jesus in the Garden of Gethsemane as the three disciples slept. And it was Mark who had the linen cloth pulled from his body and fled "naked" from the temple guards.

Incidentally, John Mark would not have to have been totally bare to be considered naked. Jews of that time wore an inner garment or *kethoneth* beneath their outer garment, or *me'yil*. This was a square or oblong piece of cloth wrapped around the body like a sheet. A man wearing only his inner garment was considered to be naked.[1] Although John Mark had his *kethoneth* on, he was considered to be "naked."

21

What Did Jesus Do Between the Cross and the Resurrection?

When Jesus was crucified, His body lay in the tomb for three days and nights. Where was the spirit of the Son of God during this time? What was Jesus doing during the three days between His death and resurrection from the dead? I believe we can find the answer to these questions in the Scriptures.

There are three possibilities for where Jesus spent this time.

1. He was in heaven.
2. He remained in the tomb.
3. He was in hell.

1. We can easily eliminate the first possibility, that Jesus was in heaven during these three days, by examining what He told Mary Magdalene after the Resurrection. She had come to the tomb early on Sunday morning to find the stone rolled away from the sepulcher. Mary had run to find the disciples, telling them that someone had taken away the body of the Lord. Peter and John had quickly come to the garden and found only the linen burial clothing in the empty tomb. Then Peter and John went back to the house where they had been staying.

But Mary had stayed near the tomb, weeping. Inside the burial chamber hewed from stone, she saw two angels. They asked why she was weeping and Mary replied it was because she did not know where the body of Jesus had been taken. Then Mary turned away and saw a man whom she supposed was the gardener. When this man spoke to her, she recognized Jesus.

Although the Scripture does not specifically tell us, we can assume that Mary tried to embrace Jesus in her joy. But Jesus would not let her, saying: "... Touch me not; for I am not yet ascended to my Father: but go to my brethren, and say unto them, I ascend unto my Father, and your Father; and to my God, and your God" (John 20:17).

Jesus, himself, tells us that he had not spent the three days in heaven, for He had not yet ascended to God. Later, after He showed himself to His disciples, He allowed them to touch His body. In fact He invited Thomas to thrust his hand into the wound in His side. But when Mary had seen Jesus early on the day in which He has arisen, He would not allow His body to be touched because He had not ascended yet to His Father. Certainly, it is abundantly clear that Jesus had not spent the past three days in heaven.

2. Did Jesus remain within the tomb? There is absolutely no doubt that Jesus was physically dead when His body was taken down from the cross. The spear which was thrust into His side resulted in both blood and water issuing from the wound. This is forensic evidence that the pericardial pleura, the membrane around the heart, had been ruptured. But physical death is not oblivion, for we know that the spirit lives on after death.

On the cross Jesus promised one of the thieves who was also being crucified: ". . . Today shalt thou be with me in paradise" (Luke 23:43).

From this it is evident that there was no soul sleep, that Jesus would not remain within the tomb until His resurrection. From this passage in Luke, some have drawn the conclusion that Jesus was instantly transported to heaven after His death, but an examination of the Greek word used here indicated that this may not be true at all. The word translated *paradise* from the Greek παραδετσος is of Oriental origin, meaning a sort of Eden.[1]

But later in the Gospel of Luke, we witness Jesus being physically taken up into heaven. "And it came to pass, while he blessed them, he was parted from them, and carried up into heaven" (Luke 24:51).

The Greek word used here and translated as *heaven* is

οὐρανος. This means the abode of God.[2] It is clear that Jesus did not ascend to heaven, the abode of His Father, from the cross. But it is also certain that He did not remain within the tomb.

3. The remaining possibility is that Jesus descended into hell during the time between the Crucifixion and the Resurrection. Can we find any substantiation in Scripture for this? Let us look at what Peter tells us. "For Christ also hath once suffered for sins, the just for the unjust, that he might bring us to God, being put to death in the flesh, but quickened by the Spirit: By which also he went and preached unto the spirits in prison; Which sometime were disobedient, when once the longsuffering of God waited in the days of Noah, while the ark was a preparing, wherein few, that is, eight souls were saved by water" (1 Pet. 3:18-20).

Peter tells us that Jesus went to preach to the spirits who were in prison, spirits of people who had been sometime disobedient. From this Scripture, Peter implies that at least some of these people lived during the time of Noah and had perished in the great Flood when God destroyed all human life on earth except Noah and his family. Is there any other Scripture which might verify this? Let us look at one of the prophecies concerning Jesus. "For thou wilt not leave my soul in hell; neither will thou suffer thine Holy One to see corruption" (Ps. 16:10).

On the day of Pentecost, Peter preached to a multitude in Jerusalem. In that sermon, Peter cited some of the prophecy concerning the coming of the Messiah. He told them of David speaking about foreseeing the Lord and quoted Psalm 16:10 which David had written a thousand years before concerning the coming Christ.

"Therefore being a prophet, and knowing that God had sworn with an oath to him, that of the fruit of his loins, according to the flesh, he would raise up Christ to sit on his throne; He seeing this before spake of the resurrection of Christ, that his soul was not left in hell, neither his flesh did see corruption. This Jesus hath God raised up, whereof we all are witnesses" (Acts 2:30-32).

Paul also wrote of what Jesus did between the Cross and the Resurrection in his letter to the church at Ephesus. "Wherefore he saith, When he ascended up on high, he led captivity captive, and gave gifts unto men. (Now that he ascended, what is it but that he also descended first into the lower parts of the earth? He that descended is the same also that ascended up far above all heavens, that he might fill all things)" (Eph. 4:8-10).

We see that Paul confirms Peter's statement that Jesus descended into the lower parts of the earth, where it was believed that hell was located, before He ascended into heaven with His Father. Peter tells us His purpose: to preach to the captives which were imprisoned there.

Now we must ask the question, for what purpose did Jesus go to preach to the dead? From Peter's writing, these were not righteous people. He describes them as being disobedient. There are two possibilities for Christ's preaching to them:

1. To mock them in telling them how wrong they had been in rejecting God.
2. To give them an opportunity to accept His sacrifice for their sins and obtain forgiveness for their sins.

To decide between these two, we must determine what the Scriptures say about the very *character* of Jesus and the purpose of His mission, the specific reason why He was sent by the Father to the people of this world. Was it to mock and degrade sinners? Of course not! It was the religious leaders who felt the bite of His tongue, not the sinner. And He told us very plainly why He had come in the Gospel of Luke. "I came not to call the righteous, but sinners to repentance" (Luke 5:32).

And who were these sinners that He came to call? "But God commendeth his love toward us, in that, while we were yet sinners, Christ died for us" (Rom. 5:8).

Does this mean that only those who were alive when Jesus arose from the dead were forgiven? Were these the only ones that He died for? Does this mean that only those who were on the earth during His lifetime are offered eternal life and forgiveness? Certainly not, for if this were true, then you and I would have no hope of salvation. Christ died, not only for those who were alive at His coming, but for *all sinners.*

This certainly means those who have lived *after* He sacrificed His life for the salvation of mankind. But could it possibly mean that this included those who had lived *before* He came to earth?

From the writings of both Peter and Paul we find that Jesus descended into the lower regions of the earth during the time between the Cross and the Resurrection. Since He clearly tells us that He came not to the righteous, but to call sinners to repentance, then He must have descended into hell *to also call sinners to repentance.*

These people included those who had scoffed at Noah. They also probably included all those who had died sinners before the time of Christ. It must have been a multitude, for Paul tells us the state of humanity. "Wherefore, as by one man sin entered into the world, and death by sin; and so death passed upon all men, for that all have sinned: (For until the law sin was in the world: but sin is not imputed when there is no law. Nevertheless death reigned from Adam to Moses, even over them that had not sinned after the similitude of Adam's transgression, who is the figure of him that was to come)" (Rom. 5:12-14).

Hardly anyone could have escaped condemnation. There must have been a huge multitude for Jesus to preach to when He descended into the lower regions. But His mission was to call *all* sinners, past, present, and future. Where were these sinners?

Jesus had promised the thief next to Him on the cross that on that very day he would be with Him in Paradise. Where was this place called Paradise? Many Jews, especially those who believed in an afterlife, thought that there was such a place where the souls of the dead rested until they were raised again on the last day.

Jesus seems to confirm this in the parable of the beggar and the rich man and where each found himself after death. The rich man, who had been evil, had been consigned to the flames of hell. But Lazarus, the beggar, was in a place called "Abraham's bosom." "And it came to pass, that the beggar died, and was carried by the angels into Abraham's bosom: the rich man also died, and was buried; And in hell he lifted up his eyes, being in torments, and seeth Abraham afar off, and Lazarus in his bosom" (Luke 16:22-23).

The rich man asked that Lazarus be allowed to dip his finger in water and come down and cool his tongue. But it was not possible for Lazarus to enter the place where the rich man languished in torment. Abraham explained to the rich man that this was impossible. He was reaping punishment for his life, just as the beggar was being comforted for living a just life. "And beside all this, between us and you there is a great gulf fixed: so that they which would pass from hence to you cannot; neither can they pass to us, that would come from thence" (Luke 16:26).

Was the beggar Lazarus in heaven? I don't believe that he was, for Jesus has also told us that there was only one door to heaven, through which men must pass to go to the Father. "Jesus saith unto him, I am the way, the truth, and the life: no man cometh unto the Father, but by me" (John 14:6).

Before Jesus came to earth, this "door" was not available. It was only after He gave His life as a sacrifice for the sins of all men that this pathway to the Father in heaven was available.

22

Christmas Day — Why the Twenty-fifth of December?

Although most Christians celebrate the twenty-fifth day of December as the birthday of Jesus Christ, few really believe that this date is the actual day of this event.

Why is this particular day observed? Who selected this day to commemorate His birth? When was it first celebrated? What is the significance of the decorated tree? Why are presents exchanged?

In order to answer these and other questions regarding Christmas, we must look at the history of the Early Church and the customs, and what life was like for ordinary people when the first believers in Jesus Christ lived in the pagan atmosphere of that time. Christians were very much in the minority. They had to live among neighbors who worshipped the many gods of the pagan world. Many suffered persecution under the edicts of the Roman emperors.

For ordinary people, both Christian and non-Christian, life was hard. There was little to break the monotony of work. Food was plain, consisting mainly of bread, fruit, and vegetables. Meat was reserved for feasts, and these were looked forward to with great anticipation. There was little amusement or diversion from a life of toil and hardship.

One of the major celebrations of that time was the Saturnalia, also called *Natalis solis invicti*, the Feast of the Invincible Sun. This was a week-long event at the time of the winter solstice. During this week there was a carnival atmosphere of unbridled merriment, which survives even today as the Mardi Gras of New Orleans. Morals were slack, there was an abundance of food and delicacies, and freedom from the daily grind of hard work. Gifts were exchanged and visits were made to the homes of friends and neighbors. It was also a time when Christians felt free from persecution.

The purpose of all this was ostensibly to appease the sun god, encouraging him to bring a return of longer days and ensure that spring would come again for the planting of crops. Since the life of a Christian was as drab as that of his neighbors, many believers participated in this holiday. This was a source of consternation to the fathers of the Early Church.

In perhaps the first instance of complying with the adage, "If you can't lick 'em, join 'em," the practice of observing the last day of the Saturnalia, December 25, as the birthday of Jesus Christ was begun sometime before the year A.D. 245. Origen wrote in that year that it was a sin to celebrate Jesus' birth, "as though he were a king Pharaoh." The first mention of December 25 as the date of the birth of Jesus is in a liturgical calendar for the year A.D. 336.[1]

Christmas Day, December 25, was first recognized as an official holiday in A.D. 354 by edict of the Roman emperor Justinian.[2] The observance began in Rome, then spread to other parts of the empire. But the Eastern church, already disputing the authority of Rome, decided to celebrate Christmas on January 6 as both the birth and baptism of Jesus.

Pagan Influence on Christmas

Although many people look upon this holiday as purely Christian, it is surprising how many of our Christmas customs are carryovers from the pagan celebration of the Saturnalia. The Romans adorned their houses with the green boughs of fir trees and holly. It was thought that ivy brought good luck, especially to women, and the combination of the holly's green leaves and red berries would ward off the "evil eye."[3]

Many ancient cultures used trees in religious celebrations. During the winter solstice the Druids hung apples on the branches of oak and fir trees to thank their god, Odin, for blessing them with fertility. They made cakes shaped like birds, fish, and animals, very similar to our Christmas cookies. Some people hung candles on the sacred trees in honor of the sun god.[4]

The practice of giving gifts on Christmas also originated with the pagan celebration of *Saturnalia*. This is not, as many believe, in remembrance of the gifts that the Magi brought to the Christ Child.

The Christian custom of decorating the Christmas tree may have originated with Martin Luther. There is a legend that while he was walking home on a clear and cold night, he saw stars shining through the fir trees. It seemed as though they had settled on the boughs, themselves. Luther, the legend says, cut a small tree and brought it home. He placed candles in metal holders on the branches of this tree.[5]

Early German Lutherans brought this custom to America which enraged the Puritans. In both England and the colonies, the Puritans were successful in banning this pagan inspired practice, but eventually the tree became a widespread symbol of Christmas.

Dutch settlers introduced Santa Claus as they migrated to America and this tradition has become thoroughly entrenched in our celebration of Christmas — replacing to a large degree the commemoration of the birth of Christ with a highly-commercialized holiday.

The celebration of Christmas was actually outlawed in England in 1644 by an act of Parliament under the influence of the Puritans. In 1659 a law was passed in the state of Massachusetts which imposed a fine on anyone who celebrated Christmas.

The popular abbreviation of Christmas to Xmas is a combination of X, the first letter in the Greek name for Jesus, and *mas*, a shortened version of mass. Literally, it means "the mass of Christ."[6] The word Christmas can be traced to 1038 and the shortened version, Xmas, to the fourteenth century.

But whatever the origins of the date we celebrate Christmas or the customs which have become tradition, it has become a national holiday and a permanent part of our culture. What is important for us to remember, however, is the real meaning of this day and what it was meant to represent in the Christian year — the commemoration of the birth of Jesus Christ.

The Origin of Easter

In the very early days of the church most Christians were converts from Judaism. Passover was still to them an ingrained and extremely important day to be observed. Since the Resurrection was just three days after the Crucifixion, which had occurred on a Passover, the church observed Easter on the fourteenth day of Nisan, the day of Passover. But when Gentiles became predominant in the Christian Church, dissension began as to which day should be observed to commemorate the resurrection of the Lord.

Gentile Christians felt that this day should be observed on a Sunday — the Lord's Day. Passover was always the fourteenth of the lunar month, no matter on which day of the week it fell. Controversy reached the boiling point, there were heated debates among church leaders, strong words were exchanged. The arguments were about to tear apart the Early Church.

We get an idea of how strong the dispute had become in the second century A.D. in the writings of Eusebius. The bishops of the churches in Asia insisted that they must observe the custom of keeping the Passover as the day of Easter. Churches elsewhere wanted Easter to be celebrated on Sunday, the Lord's Day. The Asian churches cited all of the Apostles and early martyrs who were buried in their cities and who had observed Passover in commemoration of the Resurrection. Synods and conferences of bishops were set up, and a letter was drafted by the European-led churches. This proclaimed that never on any other day except the Lord's Day should the mystery of the Lord's resurrection from the dead be celebrated. Naturally, the Eastern churches refused to accept this decree.

In 325 A.D. the emperor Constantine called the Council of Nicaea to settle this dispute. This council decided that Easter should fall on Sunday following the first full moon after the vernal equinox. The date of March 21 was chosen as the official date of the vernal equinox. This was accepted by the Eastern churches with the added stipulation that Easter must always fall after Passover. As a result, even today these Eastern churches celebrate Easter 13 days later than those in the West. Just as the Puritans opposed the celebration of

Christmas, they also did not observe Easter. As a result, the celebration of Easter was limited in America. Moravians who had immigrated to this country began in 1741 to hold sunrise services, complete with choir and band. Catholics observed the day with mass. But the widespread observance was not known until the 1870's. Only after the Civil War did the observance of Easter become a part of American tradition.[7]

Robert Meyers, writes, "Perhaps it was the deep scars of death and destruction which led the people back to the Easter season. The story of the Resurrection was a logical inspiration of renewed hope for all those bereaved by the war."[8]

The Easter Bunny, Eggs, and Other Symbols

It is rather strange that the Easter baskets parents prepare for their children contain brightly-colored hard-boiled eggs supposedly laid by a rabbit. Certainly, almost any child knows that rabbits do not lay eggs. How did this obviously false bit of biology pervade a Christian festival?

First we must understand that Easter, itself, is *not* a holiday which originated with Christianity. In fact, the name *Easter* is pagan in origin, coming from the Babylonian goddess who was known at various times as *Ostera, Astarte, and Ishtar* which was pronounced the same way as we pronounce Easter. The goddess Ishtar was also known as *Semiramis*, the wife of Nimrod who was the priest-king of Babylon. The egg story began with Semiramis.

According to Babylonian mythology, an egg of extraordinary size fell one day from the heavens and landed in the Euphrates River. Some large fish rolled this egg to shore where several doves descended from heaven and incubated it. When this egg hatched, out came Semiramis, the goddess of Easter. The egg became the symbol of fertility and is found as such in many cultures all over the world. It also became the symbol for the goddess herself.

The Babylonian legend says that when Nimrod died, he became the sun-god. His wife, Semiramis, then gave birth to a son named Tammuz, whom she claimed to be the child of the deified Nimrod and the was the "seed of the woman" promised in Genesis 3:15. Semiramis then demanded that the people worship both her son, Tammuz, and herself.

Christians will certainly recognize this Babylonian mythology as the work of Satan in attempting to counterfeit the birth of Jesus, some 2,000 years later. Because this story predates the birth of Jesus by two millennium, it also eliminates any possible connection between the Easter egg and that blessed event, the birth of our Lord.

Now about that miraculous rabbit that supposedly lays eggs!

This, too, is from a pagan myth. But to be correct, the animal should be a hare — not a rabbit. From early antiquity, the hare has been one of the symbols for the moon. Hares are born with their eyes fully open, and the Egyptian name for the hare was *Un*, meaning "open." It was thought that hares watched for the full moon with fully-opened eyes which never blinked. Just how this wide-eyed animal was credited with producing eggs is not precisely known.

In this country, the white Easter lily is also a symbol of this event in the church calendar. Many sanctuaries are decked out with these fragrant, waxy flowers. This flower, however, is not naturally a spring-blooming plant. It is only that florists have discovered how to *force* it into bloom at the Easter season that it has become a symbol of this event. The flower was found growing on an island near Japan and was taken to Bermuda. From there it was introduced into the United States.[9] This lily, however, has been revered by many pagan cultures as a fertility symbol connected with the reproductive organs.

For many Christians, the sunrise service on Easter morning is of great spiritual significance. But even this has its roots in pagan tradition. Robert Myers writes, "Sunrise services are not unrelated to the Easter fires held on the tops of hills in continuation of the New Year fires, a worldwide observance in antiquity. Rites were performed at the vernal equinox welcoming the sun and its great power to bring new life to all growing things."[10]

Although the custom of having hot-cross buns for breakfast on Good Friday has practically died out, I can well remember eating them as a young boy. What connection is there between these buns and Easter? Or to Christianity, for that matter? Again we have to look deeply into Babylonian mythology, and to our own Bible which also discusses these small cakes. "The children gather wood, and the fathers kindle the fire, and the women knead their dough, to make cakes to the queen of heaven, and to pour out drink offerings unto other gods, that they may provoke me to anger" (Jer. 7:18).

Who is this "queen of heaven" that the Hebrew women were making cakes to sacrifice to? Do you remember Semiramis, the wife of Nimrod and mother of Tammuz? Semiramis, also known as Ishtar, was the Babylonian "Queen of Heaven." This was the goddess for whom the women in Jeremiah's time were preparing the sacrificial little raisin cakes. And these small raisin cakes are the origin of the hot cross buns which are traditionally eaten on Good Friday.

The Origin of Lent

The 40-day period between Ash Wednesday and the day before Easter is a time of fasting for much of the Christian world, when those who observe Lent eat sparingly. This is eight weeks in the Eastern churches where both Saturdays and Sundays are regarded as festival days. Western churches regard only Sundays as festivals.

Lent was instituted by Rome in the sixth century, although there is some evidence that it was observed by some churches as early as the fourth century. There is no Apostolic origin for this fast, supposedly to commemorate the 40 days in which Jesus fasted in the desert before His temptation by Satan. But the Lenten fast is identified with a practice among the worshippers of Semiramis in which the death and resurrection of her son Tammuz was celebrated by an annual feast preceded by a Lenten fast.[11] This also corresponds to the length of a fast practiced by ancient Egyptians.

In any event, the observance of Lent has no real biblical basis and was not regarded by either the Apostles nor the early Christian Church.

Easter is the single most important event in the entire church year. Without the Resurrection, we as Christians would have no basis for our faith. Paul stated it well. "And if Christ be not risen, then is our preaching vain, and your faith is also vain" (1 Cor. 15:14).

But Christ is indeed risen. Our faith rests securely in it. Next Easter, let us not concentrate on the brightly-colored eggs, the chocolate bunnies, jelly beans, and other varieties of candy. Let us celebrate the most glorious event in all of history — the resurrection of the Son of God — and the promise of eternal life for each of us who acknowledge Him as Lord.

23

What Were a Jot and a Tittle?

When Jesus was speaking to the multitude as He delivered the Sermon on the Mount, He made a statement quoted in Matthew which has led many to wonder just what He was referring to. "For verily I say unto you, Till heaven and earth pass, one jot or one tittle shall in no wise pass from the law, till all be fulfilled" (Matt. 5:18).

What is a jot? What is a tittle?

From the context of the Lord's message and in how He used these expressions, it is evident that He was referring to something very small. And, in fact, He was. The Law had been written down by Moses in the language of the Jews — Hebrew. Jesus was using something very small in the written Hebrew when He referred to a "jot."

The Hebrew letter *yod* is the smallest letter in the Hebrew alphabet. It corresponds to the English letter "Y." It is little more than an extremely minute squiggle of a line, almost like the apostrophe we use when we either omit certain letters or designate possession, such as when we write don't to mean do not, or write Mary's little lamb.

The Hebrew letter *yod* is written **י**.

You can see that it takes only the slightest stroke with a pen to form this letter. But the *yod* is a very important letter in Hebrew and it certainly is important to Christians. It is the first letter in both the name of God, the Father, and the name of Jesus Christ, in Hebrew.

Jesus also mentioned a "tittle." What is a tittle?

When a person first looks at the letters of the Hebrew alphabet, many of them look so much alike that it is very difficult initially to tell the difference between many of them. This is very true of the Hebrew letters which correspond to the English letters D and R.

The Hebrew letter *dalet*, or "D" is written as ⁊.

The Hebrew letter *res*, or "R" is written ⁁.

As you can see, the only difference between these two letters is a small diagonal line added to the top of the vertical stem of the letter before the line becomes horizontal. It, too, is only a minuscule stroke of the pen, but changes the meaning of the letter from a "D" to an "R." This was called by Hebrew scholars a "little horn."

In the Greek of the New Testament, Jesus actually called the tittle the *keraia* or "little horn" when He spoke to the Pharisees. "And it is easier for heaven and earth to pass, than one tittle of the law to fail" (Luke 16:17).

The Law that Jesus was referring to was, of course, the body of commandments given by God to Moses. The cornerstone of this Law is the Ten Commandments. Jesus was telling the Pharisees — and telling us today — that He had not come to abolish this Law. It is still as much in effect today as when God first gave it to Moses on the mountain. God's Law is not, as Ted Turner has proposed, "The Ten Suggestions."

But are we today still under the old Mosaic Law? Are Gentiles required to conform to the same ordinances that strict, Orthodox Jews observe? What does Scripture have to say about that?

There had been much concern and differences of opinion in the Early Church concerning the Law of Moses and whether Gentile Christians remained bound under this Law. In his letter to the Galatian Church, Paul informs them where they stand in relation to the Law. "But before faith came, we were kept under the law, shut up unto faith which should afterwards be revealed. Wherefore the law was our schoolmaster to bring us unto Christ, that we might be justified by faith. But after that faith is come, we are no longer under a schoolmaster. For ye are the children of God by faith in Christ Jesus" (Gal. 3:23-26).

Is Paul telling us that we should no longer pay attention to the Ten Commandments? Have they been rescinded? Not at all! Do they apply to Gentiles as well as the Hebrews to which they were given? Certainly they do! God has not relaxed the moral standards under which He expects us to live.

Then what did Paul mean when he said that we no longer needed the "schoolmaster," the Law, by which to live? By the time of Jesus, the priests had forged a heavy chain of legalism which was choking the Hebrews. They had interpreted the Law in such a strict and hair-splitting fashion that it was strangling those who attempted to live under these man-made interpretations of God's law. In some cases, it was impossible to obey one point of Pharisaic legalism without breaking another. The spirit of the law had been sacrificed by imposing on the people the blind observance of the letter of the law, sometimes taken to an absurd degree.

Jesus clarified this once and for all when He was asked which of the commandments was the greatest by one of the Hebrew lawyers. His answer placed all of the man-made additions to the Law in their proper perspective. "Jesus said unto him, Thou shalt love the Lord thy God with all thy heart, and with all thy soul, and with all thy mind. This is the first and great commandment. And the second is like unto it, Thou shalt love thy neighbor as thyself. On these two commandments hang all the law and the prophets" (Matt. 22:37-40).

With these words, Jesus cut away all of the self-imposed legalism of the Pharisees. His message was plain and simple: If you love God with all of your heart, soul, and mind and treat your fellow human beings exactly as you would wish to be treated, it follows that you will also keep the spirit of the rest of God's laws of moral behavior.

A person who loves God with all his heart, soul, and mind cannot possibly place another god — be it money, pleasure, or anything else — before the Maker of the universe. Nor could that person steal, cheat, lie, or take another's life. Adultery would be unthinkable to one who loves God with all his heart, soul, and mind. That person would covet nothing belonging to someone else.

But can we human beings, in our own weak flesh, truly love God that much? Can we actually love others as ourselves? No, not in our own weak flesh! But there is another way we can find the strength to accomplish the seemingly impossible task of total love for God and for our fellowmen.

Not by our own strength, but through the limitless power of Jesus Christ.

If we confess our own weakness, our own inability to live a righteous life, and ask Jesus Christ to come into our hearts and *live His life through us*, then we can depend, not on our own righteousness, but on His, to please God. Does this mean that when we ask Jesus into our hearts we no longer sin? No, it does not. What it does mean is that when we make Jesus Christ our Lord and Saviour, we also accept the sacrifice that He made on the cross for the forgiveness of our sins.

Before the Cross there was no forgiveness under the Law. Those who lived under the Law were judged by the Law. Jesus did not remove the Law, not one "jot" nor "tittle" of the Law was changed by Jesus. But what He offers is a way of escape from being judged under the Law, for no one can *earn* salvation, it is the gift to us that Christ made when He gave His own life as a ransom for us. "For by grace ye are saved through faith; and that not of yourselves: it is the gift of God: Not of works, lest any man should boast" (Eph. 2:8-9).

We cannot earn, nor do we merit, our salvation. We cannot work our way into heaven, nor can we live good enough lives to deserve it. It is only by faith in Jesus Christ and in accepting the gift of the sacrifice He made on the Cross that we can escape being judged under the Law — and found guilty.

But with Jesus there is escape from the punishment under the Law which each one of us deserves, for we are all sinners. Accept the invitation that Jesus makes to every one of us. "Come unto me, all ye that labour and are heavy laden, and I will give you rest. Take my yoke upon you, and learn of me; for I am meek and lowly in heart: and ye shall find rest unto your souls. For my yoke is easy, and my burden is light" (Matt. 11:28-30).

Accept the offer that Jesus makes to all of us. And by doing so, get out from underneath the heavy sword of the Law, every "jot" and "tittle" of it, that hangs in condemnation over our heads.

24

The "Lost Books" of the Old Testament

Are the books which our modern Bibles contains all that were ever written? Have some books been lost? Or has God divinely protected those manuscripts which He intended for us to look upon as His Word for our edification and guidance through the millenniums since they were first written? In this chapter we will look at what some call the Bible's "lost" books.

The Lost Books

Old Testament Scripture refers to books which are completely unknown to us today. The first reference to one of these "lost" books may be found early in Israelite history. It was Moses, who is credited with writing the first five books of the Old Testament, who refers to another book, which he calls "the book of the wars of the Lord."

THE WARS OF THE LORD: We know nothing about this book. From the reference made by Moses, this book must have given details of how God fought the battles for the Israelites against their enemies during the Exodus. It is not clear whether this book was also written by Moses, or by someone else who experienced these battles. "Wherefore it is said in the book of the wars of the Lord, What he did in the Red sea, and in the brooks of Arnon, And at the stream of the brooks that goeth down to the dwellings of Ar, and lieth upon the border of Moab" (Num. 21:14-15).

Moses calls attention to what the Lord did in parting the waters of the sea when the Israelites passed safely through and the pursuing Egyptian army was drowned. He also makes note of what happened at the Brook of Arnon. It was here that Sihon the Amorite, the king of Heshbon, was given over into the hand of the Israelites when he would not allow them to peacefully pass through his land. With the help of the Lord the Israelites defeated the Amorites and destroyed the men, women, and children of the cities. Moses also mentioned the brooks which flowed down to the dwellings of Ar, in Moab. The Lord would not allow them to go into battle against the Moabites. These people were the descendants of Lot, and God had given them possession of this land.

THE BOOK OF JASHER: This book is mentioned twice in Scripture. The first reference to the book of Jasher is about the battle between the Israelites and the Amorites, and how God participated in this struggle. The kings of five Amorite cities came against the men of Gibeon. "Therefore the five kings of the Amorites, the king of Jerusalem, the king of Hebron, the king of Jarmuth, the king of Lachish, the king of Eglon, gathered themselves together, and went up, they and all their hosts, and encamped before Gibeon, and made war against it" (Josh. 10:5).

The men of Gibeon sent a message to Joshua at Gilgal asking for help. Joshua assembled his men of war and went to the aid of the Israelites of Gibeon. The Lord spoke to him, telling him not to be afraid, for the Lord would also fight against the Amorites and not a man of them would be able to stand before Joshua.

Joshua's army began a great slaughter of the Amorites and chased them all the way to Azekah and Makkedah. The Lord cast down great hailstones from heaven upon the Amorites and the Bible tells us that more of the Amorites died from the hail than were slain by the Israelites.

Joshua saw that it was possible to completely destroy this army of Amorites once and for all. The only thing that concerned him was that night might fall before he could accomplish this. Joshua asked the Lord to delay the going down of the sun until his victory could be completed. "And the sun stood still, and the moon stayed, until the people had avenged themselves upon their enemies. Is not this written in the book of Jasher? . . ." (Josh. 10:13).

This "lost" book is mentioned again about 350 years after

Joshua's battle with the Amorites when the sun did not set until his victory could be completed. The time of the judges of Israel had passed and the Israelites had asked for a king to rule over them and Saul was chosen.

The Lord selected David to succeed Saul, and in a battle with the Philistines both Saul and his son Jonathan were killed. When David heard about the death of the king, and of his friend Jonathan, he tore his clothes and put earth upon his head in grief. David became king and he had to form and train a new army to defend Israel. "And David lamented with this lamentation over Saul and over Jonathan his son: (Also he bade them teach the children of Judah the use of the bow: behold, it is written in the book of Jasher) (2 Sam. 1:17-18).

CHRONICLES OF KING DAVID: It was certainly not unusual for kings to keep records of what happened during their reign. In the Book of Esther we read that when King Ahasuerus could not sleep, he called for a servant to bring the book of records of the chronicles of his reign to be read to him. Probably all kings kept such books.

The chronicles that David kept may actually not be lost. The two books of First and Second Chronicles that we find in our Old Testaments may actually reflect those records. But in one of these, the book of the chronicles of King David is specifically mentioned. The Lord had forbade the numbering of the Israelites, but during David's reign a census was begun. Before it could be completed, the Lord's wrath fell upon Israel. "Joab the son of Zeruiah began to number, but he finished not, because there fell wrath for it against Israel; neither was the number put in the account of the chronicles of king David" (1 Chron. 27:24).

OTHER BOOKS ABOUT DAVID: Apparently there were several men who wrote down what happened during David's reign over Israel. These books are mentioned together in one verse, so there must have been several accounts kept separately. "Now the acts of David the king, first and last, behold, they are written in the book of Samuel the seer, and in the book of Nathan the prophet, and in the book of Gad the seer, With all his reign and his might, and the times that went over him, and over Israel, and over the kingdoms of the countries" (1 Chron. 29:29-30).

THE BOOK OF THE ACTS OF SOLOMON: After David,

Solomon became king of Israel. He also would have kept a record of what occurred during his reign, and this book is mentioned in Scripture. "And the rest of the acts of Solomon, and all that he did, and his wisdom, are they not written in the book of the acts of Solomon?" (1 Kings 11:41).

There must have been other accounts kept of Solomon's reign beside this book. Three other chronicles referred to were compiled by Nathan, Ahijah, and Iddo. "Now the rest of the acts of Solomon, first and last, are they not written in the book of Nathan the prophet, and in the prophecy of Ahijah the Shilonite, and in the visions of Iddo the seer against Jeroboam the son of Nebat?" (2 Chron. 9:29).

When Solomon died, his son Rehoboam succeeded him. The kingdom was divided when the northern tribes broke away and Rehoboam was left with the southern territory of Judah. He reigned for 17 years and what he did was recorded both in 2 Chronicles and in other books. "Now the acts of Rehoboam, first and last, are they not written in the book of Shemaiah the prophet, and of Iddo the seer concerning genealogies? . . ." (2 Chron. 12:15).

These books are probably the same as mentioned in 1 Kings 14:29, where they are referred to as the chronicles of the kings of Judah.

THE CHRONICLES OF THE KINGS OF ISRAEL: The northern tribes which broke away after the death of Solomon followed a man named Jeroboam who became king of Israel. Jeroboam, from the tribe of Ephraim, led the 10 northern tribes in the abandonment of the God of Abraham, Isaac, and Jacob, and installed golden bulls in the cities of Bethel and Dan, making the worship of idols the national religion of his domain.

After the death of Jeroboam, 18 kings sat upon the throne of Israel, and of 15 of these it was said that they departed not from the sins of Jeroboam. The record of these kings is also mentioned in Scripture. "And the rest of the acts of Jeroboam, how he warred, and how he reigned, behold, they are written in the book of the chronicles of the kings of Israel" (1 Kings 14:19).

There is another book mentioned in the Old Testament, but this one does not record the acts of Hebrew kings. In the Book of Esther, which tells how a Hebrew woman and her uncle saved their people from destruction during the time of the Persian empire, we find this book referred to: "And the king Ahasuerus laid a tribute upon the land, and upon the isles of the sea. And all the acts of his power and of his might, and the declaration of the greatness of Mordecai, whereunto the king advanced him, are they not written in the book of the chronicles of the kings of Media and Persia?" (Esther 10:1-2)

Although we may not have these "lost" books, our Bible probably contains the most important deeds of the men whose chronicles have been referred to in Scripture. Certainly the books of First and Second Samuel, Kings, and Chronicles reveal to us what these men were like and what they accomplished, both good and evil, during their reigns. Still, it would be most interesting to be able to read about the other incidents in the lives of these men which are not included in the Old Testament books. But perhaps God, in His infinite wisdom, has a reason for not allowing us access to them.

The Apocrypha

The books contained in the Apocrypha are not lost in the sense that they are not available. Indeed, many of these books are included in editions of today's Bibles. But many Christians know little or nothing of these books, some of which have great historical value and give us understanding of what happened during the period of time between the Testaments.

It is certainly not within the scope of this chapter to deal extensively with these books. Rather, a brief statement or summary of each will be given. If the reader desires additional information concerning the books which comprise the Apocrypha, it is readily available, as are the books themselves.

Even the meaning of the term "Apocrypha" can be confusing, arising from both the ambiguity of the ancient use of the word and the more recent application of this term to different groups of books. Etymologically (the study of the origin and use of words), the word means "things that are hidden."[1] There have been several suggestions as to why this term was applied to the books of the Apocrypha. Some say that what these books contained was too profound, too mysterious, or too difficult for any but the initiated to comprehend. Others have stated that they were to be "hidden" because they were spurious or heretical. Regardless of why this term was first applied to them, it now is the designation assigned to 15 books or portions of books.

These books are: First Esdras, Second Esdras, Tobit, Judith, the additions to the Book of Esther, the Wisdom of Solomon, Ecclesiasticus (also called the Wisdom of Jesus the Son of Sirach), Baruch, the Letter of Jeremiah, the Prayer of Azariah and the Song of the Three Young Men, Susanna, Bel and the Dragon, the Prayer of Manasseh, 1 Maccabees, and 2 Maccabees.

In addition, there are three texts which are of special interest to the Eastern Orthodox Church: 3 Maccabees, 4 Maccabees, and Psalm 151.

None of these books are found in the Hebrew canon of the Old Testament. However all with the exception of 2 Esdras were included in the Septuagint, the Greek version of the Old Testament. Since Greek was the language of many of the early Christian church fathers, they were quoted by many of these men as authoritative Scripture.

When Jerome was commissioned at the end of the fourth century by Pope Damascus to prepare a Latin version of the Bible, the Apocrypha was included with a statement that these books were in a separate category from the Hebrew canon. Later copyists of the Vulgate were not always careful to include Jerome's statement, and the Council of Trent in 1546 decreed that all of the Apocrypha except 1 and 2 Esdras and The Prayer of Manasseh were part of the Holy Scripture. Editions of the Protestant Bibles have generally not included the Apocrypha.

The books of the Apocrypha may be classified into several distinct types. 1 Esdras, 1 Maccabees, and to a degree 2 Maccabees fall into the class of historical writing. The books of Tobit, Judith, Susanna, and Bel and the Dragon are moralistic novels. The books Wisdom of Solomon and Ecclesiasticus are of a serious nature and show parallels with the Book of Proverbs. The Prayer of Manasseh, the Prayer of Azariah, and the Song of the Three Young Men are liturgical books.

The Letter of Jeremiah is an example of how this literary form might be used to convey theological ideas. Paul, of course, in the New Testament, used this type of writing with great success. Second Esdras is an apocalyptic book, purporting to reveal the future and contains many symbols involving mysterious numbers, beasts, and angelic visions reminiscent of the Book of Revelation. Baruch was purportedly written by Jeremiah's scribe and sent to Jerusalem to be read during feast days. It is a confession of Israel's guilt, the cause of the Babylonian exile, and praise to God for Israel's special gift of wisdom, and a merciful God who will restore His land.

First Esdras begins with a description of Passover celebrated by King Josiah in about 631 B.C. and represents the same incidents recorded in 2 Chronicles 35 to 36, the whole of the Book of Ezra, and part of Nehemiah. Included is an account of three young men in the court of Darius that has no parallel in the Old Testament. The purpose of the unknown author of this book was to emphasize the contribution of Josiah, Zerubbable, and Ezra in the reform of Jewish worship.[2]

Second Esdras is written so that it is Ezra who is relating his visions of the future. The Semitic original and almost all of the Greek text have been lost, but translations remain in Syriac, Coptic, Ethioptic, Arabic, Armenian, and Georgian. The entire text written later in Latin exists and appears in the Vulgate as the Fourth Book of Esdras.

The text may have been edited by an unknown Christian writer whose comments may have been included as Chapters one and two in the middle of the second century A.D. The original book is believed to have been written by a Palestinian Jew near the close of the first century A.D.[3]

This work denounces the wickedness of Rome, laments the sorrows which have fallen upon Jerusalem, and contains prophecy concerning the end of the world. Few will be saved when mankind comes before God's judgment throne which brings about the beginning of the messianic kingdom. The seer's prayer to God to "spare His people" is rejected, and God advises him not to think about the sinners who deserve their doom. There are many parallels in this book with the visions of Daniel.

Tobit is an imaginative story, set in the Assyrian capital of Nineveh, and portrays the fate of some of the people of the northern tribes of Israel after they have been taken captive. It was probably written during the second century B.C. and is derived from ancient folklore. Its value, other than being an entertaining novel, is in the picture it gives of the Jewish culture and daily life during this period.[4]

Judith is an excellent example of well-written and realistic Jewish fiction. The story revolves around the heroine, Judith, whose town of Bethulia is besieged by the Babylonian general, Holofernes. The Babylonians begin to starve the town into submission and Judith vows to save her people from destruction. She entices the general to entertain her in his tent and proceeds to get him drunk, then decapitates him.

Judith was probably written in Hebrew during the latter part of the second century B.C. and survives in Greek, two Latin versions, a Syriac version as well as several later Hebrew texts.[5]

The additions to the Book of Esther were probably made after the Hebrew Bible had been translated into Greek. It is believed that this was done by Lysimachus, an Alexandrian Jew, in about 114 B.C. A total of six additions, with 107 verses were added. It is believed that the reason these were added was to make the Book of Esther more detailed and to give a more pious flavor to the original book, which does not even mention God. In the additions, God is mentioned frequently. These additions sometimes contradict the original book of Esther and have little or no practical or historical value.[6]

The Wisdom of Solomon is purported to have been written by Solomon, but was not. It was composed originally in Greek by an unknown Hellenistic Jew sometime during the latter part of the first century B.C. Probably using traditional wisdom material, the author, who poses as Solomon, promises the reward of immortality to the righteous and warns the wicked of the judgment to come. He recalls the gift of wisdom which God bestowed on His people from Adam to Moses and warns of God's punishment on the wicked by relating His destruction of the Egyptians and Canaanites.[7]

Ecclesiasticus, or the Wisdom of Jesus the Son of Sirach, is the only book of the Apocrypha for which the author is definitely known. Joshua ben Sira was a Jewish scribe who conducted a school in Jerusalem where he lectured young men on ethical and religious subjects. In about 180 B.C. he wrote down the wisdom that he had formerly delivered orally to his students.

In about 132 B.C. his grandson translated this into Greek from the original Hebrew. In the third century A.D. the book of Sirach became known as Ecclesiasticus, or "the Church Book." The value of this book lies in that it is the last example of wisdom literature as represented by the Old Testament Book of Proverbs. It also is indicative of the school of thought that developed into the rabbinical schools of the Sadducees and Pharisees.[8]

Baruch purports to have been written during the Babylonian captivity by the man who was Jeremiah's scribe. Actually it was probably the work of at least two individuals and is assigned a date of between 150 and 60 B.C. Supposedly sent to Jerusalem by Baruch to be read on feast days, it is a confession of Israel's sin which resulted in the exile. The later part of the book consists of two poems, one praising wisdom as God's special gift to His people, Israel, and the second poem dealing with the theme of the restoration of His people. It was most probably written originally in Hebrew. The text is extant today in Greek, Latin, Syriac, Coptic, Armenian, Ethioptic, and Arabic.[9]

The Letter of Jeremiah professes to be a message sent by the prophet to the Jews who had been carried away to Babylon. In it is an impassioned plea to resist idol worship, which may be forced upon them by their captors. Also included are the author's proofs that "there are no gods" and he gives the exiles a variety of arguments against idols of silver, gold, or wood.

The Letter of Jeremiah is dated by most scholars to the Maccabean period and the original language was probably Hebrew, although some believe it may have been composed in Greek.[10]

The Prayer of Azariah and the Song of the Three Young Men are later additions to the Book of Daniel, intended to be inserted between Daniel 3:23 and 3:24. This addition has to do with the three young Hebrews, Sharach, Meshach, and Abednego who refused to worship the golden image set up by Nebuchadnezzar. Their punishment was to be thrown into the fiery furnace. The additions give Azariah's (Abednego's Hebrew name) prayer to the Lord. All three young men sing a praise song to God after they are delivered by the angel of the Lord within the furnace.

These additions date from the first or second centuries B.C. and whether they were originally composed in Hebrew, Greek, or Aramaic is debated by scholars.[11]

Susanna is another addition to the Book of Daniel and is dated to the same time as the Prayer of Azariah and the Song of the Three Young Men. This is an exceptionally well-written short story, whose heroine is cleared from a false charge of adultery by the wisdom and bravery of a young man. Since Susanna means "a lily" and Daniel means "God has judged," the names of these two characters in this story are very appropriate. The position of this addition to the Book of Daniel varies with the manuscript. In the Septuagint and Vulgate Bibles it follows the last chapter and is numbered chapter 13. Other versions sometimes use this story of Susanna as an introduction to the book of Daniel.[12]

Bel and the Dragon is another addition to the Book of Daniel and dates from the time of the previously discussed additions. In this narrative it is told of the great statue of Bel, the patron deity of Babylon, who each night devours large quantities of food and drink, thus proving itself to be a living god. Daniel discovers that it is really the priests of Bel who consume this and unmasks them as frauds.

The second part of the story tells of Daniel's refusal to worship a dragon as a god. He makes a mixture of pitch, fat, and hair and feeds it to the dragon. It dies and the priests are enraged. Daniel is sentenced to die by being cast into the lion's den. He is kept safe from the lions for six days, and fed with provisions brought from Judea by the prophet Habakkuk. On the seventh day the king removes Daniel and throws his enemies to the lions. In the Latin Vulgate, this appears as chapter 14, after Susanna.[13]

The Prayer of Manasseh is the work of an unknown Jew who decided to fill in what the account of this wicked king failed to tell us in 2 Chronicles 33:11-13. Manasseh was king of Judah for 55 years. He was 12 years old when he ascended to the throne and the Bible tells us that he did that which was evil in the sight of the Lord, ". . . like unto the abominations of the heathen, which the Lord had cast out before the children of Israel" (2 Chron. 33:2).

He even built altars to his pagan gods in the temple and

the courts of the temple, used witchcraft, caused the children to pass through the fire in the valley of Hinnom, and dealt with a familiar spirit. He was probably the most evil of all the kings of Judah, even setting up a carved idol in the house of the Lord.

When God had seen enough, He sent the Assyrians and they took Manasseh prisoner, bound him with thorns, and carried him off. This finally got the attention of the proud king. In his misery and pain, he called upon the Lord, humbling himself before the God of his fathers. God heard his prayers and restored him again to Jerusalem. The Bible tells us, ". . . Then Manasseh knew that the Lord he was God" (2 Chron. 33:13).

Manasseh had repented and when he was again king of Judah, he broke down all of the altars and high places that he had constructed, burned the carved idol, and cast out all of the pagan symbols from the city. Manasseh restored the daily sacrifices in the temple and commanded the people of Judah to serve the Lord God only and forget his former commands. What Manasseh did and the prayer that he prayed while captive of the Assyrians are referred to as being contained in one of the "lost" books.

"Now the rest of the acts of Manasseh, and his prayer unto his God, and the words of the seers that spake to him in the name of the Lord God of Israel, behold, they are written in the book of the kings of Israel" (2 Chron. 33:18).

This is the missing prayer which an unknown writer composed, perhaps to give his countrymen who had fallen into idolatry hope of forgiveness and restoration if they would also humble themselves to God as Manasseh had done.

It is difficult to date the writing of this prayer, but most scholars agree that it was probably written sometime in the last two centuries B.C. Neither are we certain of its original language; Hebrew, Greek, or Aramaic. It exists today in Greek, Latin, Syriac, Armenian, and Ethioptic. In the Vulgate Bible, it is placed in the appendix and is quite different from the original Latin translation and much more recent in origin.[14]

First Maccabees is an authentic book of history, giving us a detailed account of many of the events which occurred in the years between the Testaments. The book was probably written shortly after the death of John Hyrcanus I, the high priest from 134 to 104 B.C. It exists today in Greek, Latin, and several other languages, the original Hebrew having been lost. The author was without a doubt a Palestinian Jew who lived in Jerusalem.

This excellent book of history begins with the conquests of Alexander the Great and the establishment of his empire 336-323 B.C. It continues with the breakup of the empire and its division among Alexander's generals. The most important to the Hebrews, of course, was the Seleucid empire. Recounted are the major events of Judean history from the rise of Antiochus IV (175 B.C.) to the reign of John Hyrcanus I and the successful struggle for Jewish independence.

In essence, this is the story of Judas Maccabeus and his family and their role in the fight against the Seleucid oppression. But the writer of this book also can see the hand of God in the Maccabean victories.[15]

Second Maccabees is an abridgment of a five-volume set of history which is no longer in existence, written by a man named Jason of Cyrene. This work was an account of events in Jewish history from the time of the high priest Onias III and Seleucus IV (180 B.C.) of Syria to the defeat of Nicanor's army (161 B.C.) It parallels a portion of 1 Maccabees.

Jason's work also includes discussions of theological questions, but we are not certain that this was original or the work of the man who abridged the five-volume set. Jason's history was probably written about 110 B.C. and the abridgment made during the first century B.C. It often supplements the events cited in 1 Maccabees, but is less trustworthy in historical accuracy.[16]

Third Maccabees is not a book about the Maccabean period, but an account of the struggles of the Alexandrian Jews who suffered persecution under Ptolemy IV Philopater (221 to 203 B.C.) half a century before the Maccabean times.

The book was written in Greek in the first century B.C. by an unknown Alexandrian Jew as an attempt to exhort Egyptian Jews to hold onto their faith when they were threatened several times by Roman administration with loss of their civil status. The author cites God's miraculous intervention in preventing Ptolemy Philopater from entering the Holy of

Holies in the Jerusalem temple. After his repulsion, he returned to Alexandria with the intent of taking revenge upon the Egyptian Jews for his humiliation.

This book is valuable for its insight into the orthodox type of Judaism, devotion to temple worship, and importance of the Mosaic law, which struggled against the Hellenization of their religion by outside influences. It is not included in the Latin Vulgate, but has been accorded canonical status in the Eastern Christian churches.[17]

Fourth Maccabees is a much later expansion of 2 Maccabees, written somewhere between A.D. 20 to 54, probably in Antioch. The author was a Jew and the book is an attempt to interpret Judaism in terms of stoic Greek philosophy. It was written in Greek and is included in important manuscripts of the Greek Bible, although never formally canonized.

This book was written in praise of the Hebrew martyrs, who are described as immediately being received into heaven by the ancient patriarchs. The martyrdoms are perceived as substitutionary atonements which expiate the nation's sins and restores the land to purity. This is exemplified by the martyrdoms of Eleazar, the seven brothers, and their mother.[18]

Psalm 151 is a supernumerary psalm which is ascribed to David. It may be found in the Greek Septuagint. In this psalm, titled A Hallelujah of David the Son of Jesse, we find the Psalmist's brief description of how he was chosen by God, anointed by Samuel, and his fight against Goliath.

In 1956 a fragmentary leather scroll was found at Quamran Cave XI which contained portions of the Hebrew text of about 35 canonical psalms along with several noncanonical psalms, one of which was a somewhat enlarged form of Psalm 151.[19]

The books of the Apocrypha were the "near misses" when it came to assembling the books which were awarded canonical status and included in our Bibles. These books were not considered "inspired" and although they contained much material of substance, did not meet the high standards set for biblical inclusion. But this is not to say that these books are worthless. Indeed, 1 Maccabees provides just as much historical material of value as other books which were included in the Old Testament, although of a later period.

But in reading the books of the Apocrypha, I cannot but commend those whose task it was to choose, with divine help, the books which are in our modern Bibles. They chose well, and with the leading of the Holy Spirit, I believe the proper books were indeed chosen.

The books of the Apocrypha were not the only extra-biblical material available at that time. There were numerous other writings, not considered to be of the same status as the Apocrypha, but otherwise interesting and useful. We will now look briefly at some of these books, called by a strange and somewhat forbidding name. These books are called the *pseudepigrapha.*

The Pseudepigrapha

This term, pseudepigrapha (pronounced soo-da-pig-ra-fa), actually means "false writings," that is, writings attributed to someone who did not write them. Some of the books we will discuss here are true "pseudepigrapha" in that they have been written in the name of an Old Testament personality. Examples are 1 Enoch, the Apocalypse of Baruch, and the Testament of the Twelve Patriarchs. It should be noted, however, that several of the books of the Apocrypha also fall into this category, such as the Wisdom of Solomon, 2 Esdras, and the Letter of Jeremiah.

It is not within the scope of this chapter to look at all of the books which fall into this classification in detail. The purpose is to call the reader's attention to the fact that such books do exist, and are available for study. There are several, however, which deserve special mention.

The Book of Enoch was apparently in use by the Apostles and regarded with considerable esteem. In fact, Jude quotes from this book. "And Enoch also, the seventh from Adam, prophesied of these, saying, Behold, the Lord cometh with ten thousands of his saints" (Jude 14).

The Book of Enoch ostensibly contains Enoch's testimony of how, after God had taken him to heaven, he was shown everything from the creation of the world to the coming of the messianic period. This is truly an apocalyptic book, paralleling somewhat the Book of Revelation in the New Testament. Especially interesting is the judgment of the fallen angels.

This book contains three parables which have to do with the judgment of the world, but with the righteous having hope in the coming of the Messiah. It also contains some astronomical sections and a collection of miscellaneous exhortations. The later portion of the book divides the history of the world into 10 weeks, with the last three being apocalyptic. The oldest sections of this book date to the Maccabean period.

This book is valuable for studies of Jewish thought in the period of pre-Christian theology. Of all the books belonging to what is called the pseudepigrapha, this is without a doubt the most important.

The Letter of Aristeas is allegedly a letter written by Aristeas, a high official in the court of Ptolemy II in Alexandria. It was sent to Philocrates, supposedly Aristeas' brother in Jerusalem, relating how the Septuagint was written. This interesting, if fictional, story tells how Demetrius of Phalerum, head of the great library of Alexandria, suggested to Ptolemy that a translation be made of the Hebrew law.

The king, it is said, wrote to Eleazar the high priest in Jerusalem with a request that 72 scribes accomplish this task. The king sent rich gifts along with his request, and when the scribes arrived in Alexandria they were plied with gifts, feted at fabulous banquets, and sent to the island of Pharos to work on the translation. Each day Demetrius compared their work and wrote a consensus. The task was completed in 72 days.

The 72 translators were sent home bearing expensive gifts in appreciation for their effort. When the Greek translation of the Law was read to the king, he was greatly impressed. He expressed amazement that it had not been mentioned in earlier Greek literature. The Alexandrian Jews lauded the work and the Septuagint, Greek for the number 72, became the "Bible" of the Jews of the diaspora.

Although it is obvious that the Letter of Aristeas is fiction, it is valuable for the insight that it gives on the Hebrew custom and thought of that period. Its purpose was to commend the Jewish law to the Hellenized Gentile world. Unfortunately, it also states that the God of the Jews is the same as the one worshipped by the Greeks. God is really Zeus, with only a different name. Dating this work is almost impossible, with opinions varying from 200 to 63 B.C.

The Martyrdom of Isaiah contains the legend of the death of Isaiah. This book states that the prophet was "sawn asunder" by use of a wood saw. It dates from about the third century B.C.

The Apocalypse of Abraham is preserved in a Slavic version and was probably originally written in Hebrew after the fall of Jerusalem in A.D. 70. The first portion of the book relates how Abraham was converted to belief in God from his former pagan religion. The second part is Abraham's vision of the fall of man, the final division of the world's people into Jews and heathens, and the troubles which precede the messianic age. The Messiah, who is called the Elect One, gathers Israel into His kingdom and destroys the heathen with fire.

The Testimony of Abraham was probably written originally in Hebrew in the first or second century A.D. It exists now in Greek and scholars disagree whether it is a Christian work or Jewish with Christian interpolations.

It tells the story of Michael coming to announce to Abraham that he is about to die. Abraham then begs to be shown the world and all created things before he dies. Michael then conducts him to heaven where Abraham sees both paradise and hell, and the judgment of souls to determine which place will be their final destination. This, however, is only a preliminary judgment by Abel. At the last day, God will make the final judgment. In this story there is no Messiah, no Resurrection, and no messianic kingdom.[20]

The Sibylline Oracles were produced in about 140 B.C. by an Alexandrian Jew in imitation of the ancient Greek oracles of Sybil, a pagan prophetess. Later numerous additions were made to these and there appears to have been a total of fifteen books, twelve of which are still extant, written between the second century B.C. and the fifth century A.D.

The Jewish writer makes the oracle commend monotheism, the Mosaic laws, and other important features of Judaism.[21] By doing this, he hopes to make the pagans more receptive to Judaism. He also makes Sybil a descendant of Noah.

The Testament of the Twelve Patriarchs is based on Genesis where Jacob gives his sons instructions and teaching. This book was a Pharisaic work written toward the end of the second century B.C. and later expended by additions. There appears to be similarities with the teachings of Jesus, for example exhortations to humility, almsgiving, and brotherly love.

These may have been later additions by Christians.

The Book of Jubilees also is based on Genesis. The author advocates a 365-day year in order that the Jews accurately keep the feasts and holy days. The book purports to be a revelation given to Moses on Mt. Sinai and the purpose of the book is to affirm the eternal validity of the Mosaic law.

It was written by an unknown Pharisee somewhere during the later part of the second century B.C. in an attempt to counter the spread of Greek thought and culture among the Jews. In the course of the many revelations contained in this book, there is one of special interest: that it was Satan and not God that suggested to Abraham to sacrifice Isaac.[22]

There are a great many other books in what is called the pseudepigrapha. To list a few that may be of interest: Joseph and Asenath, Lives of the Prophets, Life of Adam and Eve, 5 Maccabees, 3 Baruch, Psalms of Joshua, The Psalms of Solomon, The Testament of Job, Paralipomena of Jeremiah the Prophet, The Secrets of Enoch, and The Assumption of Moses.

For those interested in further reading on this subject, the following book is highly recommended: *The Old Testament Pseudepigrapha: Volume I, Apocalyptic Literature and Testaments;* Edited by James H. Charlesworth; published by Doubleday & Co., Garden City, NY; 1983.

Chapter One

[1]Robert W. Faid, *A Scientific Approach to Biblical Mysteries* (Green Forest, AR: New Leaf Press, 1993).

[2]Ernst Mayr, *Principles of Systematic Zoology* (New York, NY: McGraw Hill, 1969), page 11-12.

[3]Tim LaHaye and John D. Morris, *The Ark on Ararat* (Nashville, TN: Thomas Nelson, 1976), page 247.

[4]LaHaye and Morris, *The Ark on Ararat*, page 248.

[5]Robert Rogers, *Cuneiform Parallels to the Old Testament* (New York, NY: Eaton & Mains, 1912), page 112.

[6]Isaac Preston Cory, *Ancient Fragments* (London, W. Pickering, 1832), 2nd edition, page 54.

[7]William Whiston, translator, *Complete Works of Flavius Josephus, Antiquity of the Jews* (Grand Rapids, MI: Kregal Publications, 1978), book 1, chapter 3, section 6.

[8]Whiston, *Complete Works of Flavius Josephus, Antiquity of the Jews,* book 20, chapter 2, section 2.

[9]Marcus Dods, translator, *Ante-Nicene Fathers, 1885,* volume 2, page 117.

[10]John Montgomery, *The Quest for Noah's Ark* (Minneapolis, MN: Bethany Fellowship, 1972), page 72-76.

[11]Marco Polo, *Travels of Marco Polo,* translated by Marsden (New York, NY: The Modern Library, 1926), page 25.

[12]Rev. S. Baring-Gould, *Legends of the Patriarchs and Prophets* (New York, NY: Hurst & Co.), page 142.

[13]LaHaye and Morris, *The Ark on Ararat*, page 56-58.

[14]Richard Bright, *The Ark, A Reality?* (Guilderland, NY: Ranger Associates, Inc., 1989).

[15]LaHaye and Morris, *The Ark on Ararat*, page 233-236.

Chapter Two

[1]Andson F. Rainey, *Biblical Archaeology Review,* vol. XI, no. 4, July/August 1985.

[2]Werner Keller, *The Bible as History* (New York, NY: William Morrow & Co., 1956), page 118.

[3]Herbert Lockyer, *All the Men of the Bible* (Grand Rapids, MI: Zondervan Publishing House, 1958), page 270.

[4]Keller, *The Bible as History*, page 212.

[5]"David Found at Dan," *Biblical Archaeology Review,* volume 20, number 2, March/April 1994.

[6]Andre Lemaire, " 'House of David' Restored in Moabite Inscription," *Biblical Archaeology Review,* volume 20, number 3, May/June 1994.

Chapter Four

[1]Geoffrey W. Bromiley, editor, *International Standard Bible Encyclopedia* (Grand Rapids, MI: Eerdmans Publishing Co., 1980), page 867.

[2]Bromiley, *International Standard Bible Encyclopedia*, page 184.

[3]Michael Grant, translator, *Tacitus; The Annals of Imperial Rome* (New York, NY: Penguin Books, 1956), page 157.

[4]Whiston, *Complete Works of Flavius Josephus, Antiquities of the Jews*, book XVIII, chapter 4, sections 1, 3.

[5]F.L. Cross, editor, *Oxford Dictionary of the Christian Church* (London, Oxford Press, 1958), page 1072.

[6]Merrill C. Tenney, editor, *The Zondervan Pictorial Bible Dictionary* (Grand Rapids, MI: Zondervan Publishing House, 1967), page 657.

[7]James I. Packer, Merrill C. Tenney, and William White Jr., editors, *The Bible Almanac* (Nashville, TN: Thomas Nelson, 1980), page 753.

[8]Bromiley, *International Standard Bible Encyclopedia*, page 869.

[9]Bromiley, *International Standard Bible Encyclopedia*, page 184.

Chapter Five

[1]J.D. Douglas, editor, *New Bible Dictionary* (Grand Rapids, MI: Eerdman's Publishing Co., 1962), page 116.

[2]Joseph L. Gardner, editor, *Atlas of the Bible* (Pleasantville, NY: Reader's Digest Association, 1981), page 50, 116.

[3]Aubrey de Selincourt, translator, *Herodotus, The Histories* (New York, NY: Penguin Books, Ltd., 1983), page 181.

[4]Douglas, *New Bible Dictionary*, page 116-117.

[5]Faid, *A Scientific Approach to Biblical Mysteries*, page 101.

[6]William F. Allman, "The Mother Tongue," *U.S. News & World Report*, November 5, 1990, page 65.

[7]Faid, *A Scientific Approach to Biblical Mysteries*, page 11.

Chapter Six

[1]Douglas, *New Bible Dictionary*, page 1226.

[2]Kaari Ward, editor, *ABC's of the Bible* (Pleasantville, NY: Reader's Digest Association, 1991), page 251.

[3]Douglas, *New Bible Dictionary*, page 1226.

Chapter Seven

[1]Bernard F. Batto, "Red Sea or Reed Sea," *Biblical Archaeology Review*, volume x, number 4, July/August 1994.

[2]Batto, "Red Sea or Reed Sea," *Biblical Archaeology Review*.

[3]Keller, *The Bible as History*, page 125.

[4]Keller, *The Bible as History,* page 128.
[5]"Computer Takes on the Bible," *St. Louis Post Dispatch,* March 12, 1992.

Chapter Eight

[1]Keller, *The Bible as History,* page 128.
[2]Ward, *ABC's of the Bible,* pages 139-140.
[3]Mark S. Hoffman, editor, *The World Almanac* (New York, NY: Pharos Books, 1989), page 487.
[4]James Strong, *Strong's Exhaustive Concordance of the Bible* (Peabody, MA: Hendrickson Publishers).

Chapter Nine

[1]Ephraim Isaac, "Is the Ark of the Covenant in Ethiopia?" *Biblical Archaeology Review,* volume 19, number 4, July/August 1993.
[2]Isaac, *Biblical Archaeology Review.*
[3]Graham Hancock, *The Sign and the Seal: The Quest for the Lost Ark of the Covenant* (New York, NY: Crown, 1992).

Chapter Ten

[1]"Breakthroughs in Medicine," *Discover Magazine,* June 1993.
[2]Stephen S. Morse and Robert D. Brown, "The Enemy Within," *Modern Maturity,* June/July 1993.
[3]Morse and Brown, *Modern Maturity.*
[4]Jacob Milgrom, "You Shall Not Boil a Kid in It's Mother's Milk," *Bible Review,* volume 1, number 3, Fall 1985.
[5]*Science News,* volume 130, number 24, December 13, 1986.

Chapter Twelve

[1]Henry Snyder Gehman, editor, *Westminster Dictionary of the Bible* (Philadelphia, PA: The Westminster Press, 1970), page 967.
[2]Gehman, *Westminster Dictionary of the Bible,* page 968.
[3]James Hastings, editor, *Dictionary of the Bible* (New York, NY: Charles Scribner's Sons, 1963), page 1020.
[4]Hastings, *Dictionary of the Bible,* page 1020.

Chapter Thirteen

[1]Hastings, *Dictionary of the Bible,* page 928.
[2]Hastings, *Dictionary of the Bible,* page 929.
[3]Hastings, *Dictionary of the Bible,* page 929.
[4]Hastings, *Dictionary of the Bible,* page 930.

Chapter Fourteen

[1]Hastings, *Dictionary of the Bible,* page 902.
[2]Douglas, *New Bible Dictionary,* page 1172.

[3]*Biblical Archaeology Review*, volume 19, number 4, July/August 1993, page 62.

Chapter Fifteen

[1]Gehman, *Westminster Dictionary of the Bible*, page 357.

[2]Hastings, *Dictionary of the Bible*, page 359.

[3]Merrill F. Unger, *Unger's Bible Handbook* (Chicago, IL: Moody Press, 1966), page 367.

[4]Whiston, *Complete Works of Flavius Josephus, Antiquities of the Jews*, book viii, 7:3.

[5]Whiston, *Complete Works of Flavius Josephus, Antiquities of the Jews*, book xvi, 7:1.

[6]Hastings, *Dictionary of the Bible*, page 357, 359.

[7]Gehman, *Westminster Dictionary of the Bible*, page 357.

[8]Hastings, *Dictionary of the Bible*, page 359-360.

[9]Joseph Laffan Morse, editor, *Funk & Wagnall's Standard Reference Encyclopedia* (New York, NY: Standard Reference Works Publishing Co., 1967), page 4388.

Chapter Sixteen

[1]Hastings, *Dictionary of the Bible*, page 1032.

[2]Gehman, *Westminster Dictionary of the Bible*, page 631.

[3]Bromiley, *International Standard Bible Encyclopedia*, page 1046.

[4]Bromiley, *International Standard Bible Encyclopedia*, page 1049.

[5]Hastings, *Dictionary of the Bible*, page 1035.

[6]Hastings, *Dictionary of the Bible*, page 1033.

[7]Bromiley, *International Standard Bible Encyclopedia*, page 1055.

[8]Gehman, *Westminster Dictionary of the Bible*, page 630.

[9]Aubrey de Selincourt, translator, *The Histories; Herodotus of Halicarnassus* (New York, NY: Penguin Books, Ltd., 1954), page 80.

[10]Gehman, *Westminster Dictionary of the Bible*, page 985.

[11]Cornelius Tacitus, translated by Michael Grant, *The Annals of Imperial Rome* (New York, NY: Penguin Books, 1956), page 44.

[12]Gehman, *Westminster Dictionary of the Bible*, page 631.

[13]Gehman, *Westminster Dictionary of the Bible*, page 632.

Chapter Seventeen

[1]Packer, Teeney, White, *The Bible Almanac*, page 158.

[2]Douglas, *New Bible Dictionary*, page 981.

[3]Whiston, *Complete Works of Flavius Josephus, Antiquities of the Jews*, book XIII, 14:2.

[4]Whiston, *Complete Works of Flavius Josephus, Antiquities of the Jews*, book XVII, 2:4.

[5]Packer, Teeney, White, *The Bible Almanac*, page 507.

[6]Douglas, *New Bible Dictionary*, page 1124.

[7]Whiston, *Complete Works of Flavius Josephus, Antiquities of the Jews*, book XVIII, 2:4.

[8]Packer, Teeney, White, *The Bible Almanac*, page 507.

[9]Whiston, *Complete Works of Flavius Josephus, Antiquities of the Jews*, book XIII, 8:2.

[10]Packer, Teeney, White, *The Bible Almanac*, page 507.

[11]Whiston, *Complete Works of Flavius Josephus, Antiquities of the Jews*, book II, 8:2.

[12]Douglas, *New Bible Dictionary*, page 391.

[13]C.D. Yonge, translator, *The Works of Philo; Philo Judaeus; Every Good Man Is Free* (Peabody, MA: Hendrickson, 1993), page 682-691.

[14]Douglas, *New Bible Dictionary*, page 392.

[15]Douglas, *New Bible Dictionary*, page 1151.

[16]Douglas, *New Bible Dictionary*, page 982.

Chapter Nineteen

[1]Pat Alexander, editor, *The Lion Encyclopedia of the Bible* (Herts, England: Lion Publishing; Pleasantville, NY: Reader's Digest Edition, 1987), page 139.

[2]William Sanford La Sor, "Discovering What Jewish Miqva'ot Can Tell Us About Christian Baptism," *Biblical Archaeology Review*, volume XII, Jan./Feb. 1987.

[3]Mainonides, *Book of Cleanness*, Yad, Mikva'ot, 1:7.

[4]La Sor, *Biblical Archaeology Review*, page 57-58.

[5]Ward, *ABC's of the Bible*, page 73.

[6]La Sor, *Biblical Archaeology Review*, page 52.

Chapter Twenty

[1]Packer, Tenney, and White, *The Bible Almanac*, page 480.

Chapter Twenty-one

[1]*Strong's Exhaustive Concordance*, Greek Dictionary supplement, word no. 3857.

[2]*Strong's Exhaustive Concordance*, Green Dictionary supplement, word no. 3772.

Chapter Twenty-two

[1]Ward, *ABC's of the Bible*, page 93.

[2]Keller, *The Bible as History*, page 394.

[3]David A. Ingraham, "Where Is Christ in Christmas?" *The Gospel Truth*, December 1992.

[4]Ingraham, *The Gospel Truth*, December 1992.

[5]Betty Nickerson, *Celebrate the Sun* (Philadelphia/New York: J.B. Lippincott Co., 1969), page 112.

[6]Ward, *ABC's of the Bible*, page 93.

[7]G.A. Williamson, translator, *The History of the Church, Eusebius* (New York, NY: Penguin Books, 1983), page 231-234.

[8]Robert Meyers, *Celebrations: The Complete Book of American Holidays* (Garden City, NY: Doubleday & Co., 1972), page 104.

[9]Edna Barth, *Lilies, Rabbits, and Painted Eggs: Story of the Easter Symbols* (New York, NY: The Seabury Press, 1970), page 51.

[10]Russel K. Tardo, *Rabbits, Eggs, and Other Easter Errors* (Arabi, LA: Faithful Word Publications), page 13-14.

[11]David A. Ingraham, "Rain on Your Easter Parade," *The Gospel Truth*, April 1993.

Chapter 24

[1]Herbert G. May and Bruce M. Metzger, editors, *The New Oxford Annotated Bible with the Apocrypha* (NY: Oxford University Press, 1977), page xi.

[2]May and Metzger, *The New Oxford Annotated Bible*, page 1

[3]May and Metzger, *The New Oxford Annotated Bible*, page 23.

[4]May and Metzger, *The New Oxford Annotated Bible*, page 63.

[5]May and Metzger, *The New Oxford Annotated Bible*, page 76.

[6]May and Metzger, *The New Oxford Annotated Bible*, page 96.

[7]May and Metzger, *The New Oxford Annotated Bible*, page 102.

[8]May and Metzger, *The New Oxford Annotated Bible*, page 128.

[9]May and Metzger, *The New Oxford Annotated Bible*, page 198.

[10]May and Metzger, *The New Oxford Annotated Bible*, page 205.

[11]May and Metzger, *The New Oxford Annotated Bible*, page 209.

[12]May and Metzger, *The New Oxford Annotated Bible*, page 213.

[13]May and Metzger, *The New Oxford Annotated Bible*, page 216.

[14]May and Metzger, *The New Oxford Annotated Bible*, page 219.

[15]May and Metzger, *The New Oxford Annotated Bible*, page 221.

[16]May and Metzger, *The New Oxford Annotated Bible*, page 263.

[17]May and Metzger, *The New Oxford Annotated Bible*, page 294.

[18]May and Metzger, *The New Oxford Annotated Bible*, page 309.

[19]May and Metzger, *The New Oxford Annotated Bible*, page 330.

[20]Hastings, *Dictionary of the Bible*, page 1041.

[21]Bromiley, *International Standard Bible Encyclopedia*, page 1043.

[22]Douglas, *New Bible Dictionary*, page 1060-1061.